Can the spirits of those who have made the transition called "Death" impress their voices on magnetic tape and bring through verifiable messages?

Sarah Estep believes they can and do, and that she has proved it, time and again, in the extensive, dedicated research she has carried out through the years!

"Voices on tape that shouldn't be there, voices that claim to be the dead, voices that anyone can hear . . . Sarah Estep's account of her pioneering research into Electronic Voice Phenomena is made all the more compelling by her straight forward, down to earth reportage. She is no sensationalist, but her results *are* sensational. And the best part is, you don't have to take her word for it. Estep gives step-by-step instructions so you can try recording voices on your own.

"If you've ever wondered what happens when you die, if you've lost a loved one, if you have a shred of curiosity about life and death, please read VOICES OF ETERNITY—for once a genuine breakthrough."

Sheila Ostrander & Lynn Schroeder
Authors of *Psychic Discoveries Behind the Iron Curtain, Superlearning, Handbook of Psi Discoveries, Executive ESP*

VOICES
OF
ETERNITY

Sarah Wilson Estep

FAWCETT GOLD MEDAL • NEW YORK

To Harold Sherman
Friend and mentor.
Who encouraged and showed
Faith and trust
When both were needed.
This book is dedicated with love
To his living memory.

1898–1987

Plus Ultra—There is more beyond.

Contents

Foreword

THIS IS A CHALLENGING BOOK

Can the spirits of those who have made the transition called death impress their voices on magnetic tape and bring through verifiable messages?

Sarah Estep believes they can and do, and that she has proved it, time and again, in the extensive, dedicated research she has carried out through the years.

This is a book that everyone interested in the possibility of communicating with a departed loved one will want to read.

In it, Mrs. Estep has given a frank, painstakingly honest, and comprehensive report of her experiences. She relates how she began experimenting with the tape recording of spirit voices; the problems with the static interference from what electronics experts call "white sound," which kept her from hearing and interpreting many spirit voices; the methods she found most helpful—methods that should be equally helpful to others seeking to bring through verifiable messages from those who have "gone on."

Sarah lists many fragmentary thoughts exactly as they were received. She makes no extravagant claims, does not try to dramatize. She lets you sit beside her and experience with her, her successes and disappointments as she has tried to lift the level of her communications above what seems to be the constant calls of "earthbound spirits" for help.

After long hours and months of recordings and playbacks, she has begun to gather a collection of what she terms "grade A" spirit voices, many replying in answer to her questions, and some identifying themselves as friends and loved ones. When a voice breaks through the barrier and overrides the static, it can be startling and meaningful. These are rewarding moments after long, tedious hours spent trying to hear and interpret what is being recorded.

The level of communication may be lifted when receiving instruments are more refined and capable of elimination or reduction of "white sound," and a way is found to energize or amplify the voice projection.

Sarah Estep explains it all so plainly that beginners can be given a running start in their attempts to join the research. There seems to be no question that breakthroughs in this form of so-called spirit communication are coming—and, when they do, recognizable contacts with friends and loved ones may be possible.

Harold Sherman
Sensitive and Founder
ESP Research Associates
Foundation

Chapter 1—Is It Possible?

Any unexplained phenomenon passes through three stages before the reality of it is accepted. During the first stage, it is considered laughable. During the second stage, it is adamantly opposed. Finally, during the third stage, it is accepted as self-evident.
                                        —Arthur Schopenhauer

The thought that we can communicate verbally through our tape recorder with those who have died is beyond the comprehension of many. The very implausibility of doing such a thing, coupled with its simplicity, has kept most people from trying. It is a concept almost too startling to grasp.

Many ideas throughout history have been discarded as being too ridiculous to merit further study. Less than a hundred years ago many people believed humans would never fly. Now we have gone to the moon and back. Spaceflights, atomic energy, and medical transplants belonged to the realm of science fiction. Now they are realities. Speaking with those who have gone on to another existence is one area of study ripe for further exploration.

Through the centuries many discoveries that have profoundly influenced human life seem to have come about almost by accident. Others occur as a result of dedicated work and research. In nearly every case the seemingly impossible has, in time, become possible.

When I first heard about recording voices of the dead on tape, my initial reaction was utter disbelief. As a psychical investigator, I have encountered some fraud and a great deal of self-delusion. While more people are deluded than fraudulent, whatever their claim is based upon, the end result is often the same: In most situations there is no proof of paranormal activity.

My longing to know the truth about this life, this world, and the possibility of what may lie beyond made me hesitate to summarily dismiss the claim of voice recordings. I learned that well-known, reputable people had either taken part in experiments or heard voice tapes and were favorably impressed. Although not all are agreed on the interpretation of the messages received or on the origin of the voices, most admit that they cannot be explained in normal physical terms.

Some notable individuals who have been involved with voice recordings include Professor Walter Uphoff and his wife, Mary Jo, authors and psychical investigators; A. P. Hale, physicist and electronics engineer; Olga Worrall, who before her death was an internationally known healer; the late Harold Sherman, sensitive and author; and writers Raymond Bayless, Hans Holzer, D. Scott Rogo, and Susy Smith.

In the October 1920 issue of *Scientific American*, Thomas Edison revealed that he was working on a means to communicate with the deceased. He theorized that if a person survived death, that person would be able to affect matter in some way. As a result, he was trying to design an instrument so sensitive, it would respond to the slightest movement of a discarnate entity. Steinmetz and Tesla, two other pioneers in electricity, agreed that it should be possible, theoretically, to communicate with other dimensions.

Why does humankind yearn to communicate with those who have died? For some it is difficult to face the idea of an eventual total end in a relationship with one we love. Others want confirmation that death does not mean the annihilation of our own personality. The Christian Church is reassuring in this matter. There are few religions that do not teach some form of survival after death as one of their major precepts. For many people, however, this is not enough; they are compelled to search for proof. Too often this exploration is doomed to end in disappointment and failure.

My own quest for answers about life and death began at the age of seven. Many investigators in the area of possible death survival have in their background a traumatic experience in relation to death. So it was for me.

Several years after my grandmother died, my grandfather

married a woman who, with her son, directed a funeral home in Upstate New York. Twice a year we would visit them for a few days at a time, staying with them in the funeral home where they lived. The grieving friends and relatives who came to view their loved ones in the parlor distressed me, but more than that was the horror I couldn't begin to express as I looked at those bodies lying in their caskets. It was not that the dead frightened me. Indeed, I would have been far better off if they had. It would have shown I believed that they were still capable of enough life to affect something. When no one was around, I would creep into the room and stand silently beside those stretched out before me. I knew that the dead were truly dead. They could no longer hurt anyone. Their utter stillness in the quiet room convinced me that there was little hope of heaven or hell. I realized that it was death itself, that eventually someday I, too, would lie in a similar place, that I could not bear. From then on, all life became very dear to me.

After many years, I became a psychical investigator. Still having little hope that humans survived death, I began my research by looking into the area of reincarnation. It is not surprising that I did, for I felt that if one reincarnates then one must obviously survive one's own death. There is a large amount of information suggestive of reincarnation available for study, but in most of the case histories there is usually something that prohibits those who are cautious from saying "Reincarnation is a fact!" My own work in the area bears this out. Some of the children and adults with whom I worked seemed to have memories of previous lives. A few retained strong behavioral characteristics apparently carried over from another life. But we could go only so far together. In time we would come to a barrier that couldn't be surmounted and, while the individuals with whom I was working may have been convinced they had been reincarnated, I was always left with some doubt of the genuineness of the experience.

I had just finished work with yet another child who, like the others, had not completely convinced me she had lived a previous life. At loose ends, I came across the book *Handbook of Psi Discoveries* by Sheila Ostrander and Lynn Schroeder. There are two chapters in this book devoted to voice phenomena and, in spite of finding the concept incredible, my interest grew.

If I could get voices to speak to me on tape, no matter what they said or how briefly, I felt it would give me something concrete with which to work. As I learned more about the phenomena, one thing that appealed to me was that it didn't seem necessary for the experimenter to be a medium or a psychic superstar. Almost anyone could do it, given a certain amount of equipment and the proper degree of perseverance. I felt qualified on both counts. My equipment was limited to an old tape recorder, a microphone that whistled at inconvenient times, and headphones in which the right earpiece was dead. Over the years I have learned to persist even though it might at times have been the better part of wisdom to give up gracefully.

So I started my experiments. At the beginning I had decided to give it one week: if nothing was heard by the seventh day, I would forget the whole thing. Each morning I recorded for two hours, followed by an additional two hours late at night. Because I had read in *Handbook of Psi Discoveries* that short recordings were best, I divided each two-hour period into five-minute segments. With the tape recorder recording, I would ask, "Is anyone here?" After allowing a minute for a response, if there was going to be one, I would then ask, "Who is here?" and after another minute I'd ask my final question, "Where are you?" I would allow the tape to run one more minute, then switch off the machine. The person doing the taping doesn't know until the recording is played back whether anything has come through, so each playback was begun with some excitement, but not a great deal of hope. By the fourth day I was so thoroughly bored, it was all I could do to stay awake during my ten-to-midnight stint. All that kept me going was the commitment I had made to myself to see this through for seven days. Finally, on the morning of the sixth day, I stopped asking the same three questions. If anyone was listening, I reasoned, that person must be as bored as I was. For the first time I asked, "What is your world like?" A short time later, when I played the tape back, I heard a clear voice answer my question about another world with the word *"Beauty."* Contact had been made!

In spite of the joy I felt and my belief that *"Beauty"* had come through paranormally, I was not convinced that it had originated from the dimension many call the spirit world. Could it have gotten on the tape by some other means? I decided to study the phenomena thoroughly and continue experimenting and learning as much as possible about the electronic voice.

I had never before taken part in any experiments in the area of postmortem survival. I had always been the person others told their stories to. I had none to tell myself. Now because of the "Beauty" message, I was going to become involved.

It is astounding to receive any communication from another dimension. Even hearing raps, which many people who sit in séance circles have reported, boggles the mind. How much more startling if the unseen can come through with even one word on recording tape! Most messages, I discovered, are faint, whispery voices I call Class C. Headphones must be worn to hear them, and rarely can all the words be interpreted. Class B messages are louder and clearer and can often be heard without headphones. Class A voices are the most gratifying. Loud and clear, they can be duplicated onto other tapes. No headphones are required.

Frequently at the beginning I would go for days without recording a paranormal voice. Then, when I felt most discouraged and wondered if I wanted to keep on taping, someone would speak. Now, twelve years and twenty-four-thousand messages later, I am convinced that I am in communication with entities from other dimensions. At the same time, I feel I have learned a considerable amount about life in the beyond.

Those who speak to me have expressed feelings of joy and sadness. Most have been surprised at what they found. They contribute, on their own, totally unexpected yet meaningful comments. My direct questions are frequently answered. At times I have been spoken to in German and French, two languages of which I have no knowledge. Fortunately I wrote these messages phonetically in my log and later bought German and French dictionaries. Some of the messages I was able to translate, and, once translated, they made sense. They were answers to my questions. Musical chords and notes have been played at my request. I have been told that I am loved and also that I am hated. I have been assured of their support, their protection, their help. They have asked me for help. I have been called a fool. They have said I am tested. I have been told they treasure me, that they count on me. They call me by name, even mispronouncing my last name at times just as some of my earthplane fellows do when meeting me for the first time. My life has been threatened. I have been told they look after me, that they walk with me. They show an acute awareness of me as an individual, of my strengths and weaknesses. On several occasions I have received precognitive information from the voices.

Friends and loved ones have come through, called me by name, and told me how things are for them now. For example, I had told a beloved aunt a few months before she died about my work. She was searching for reassurance that her imminent demise would not be the end, and I felt I could give her this. As she and I discussed my work her fear subsided somewhat, and she said she would try to get through to me from the other side. She has communicated, and what came through as she lay dying helps confirm the findings of those who work in the area of deathbed observations.

People I have never known have spoken to me once or twice through the tape recorder before continuing on their way, never to be heard from again. Others, taking a more active part, have stayed and come through frequently. Styhe is such an individual. He spoke one morning on tape, after I had been recording for almost one year. I had often asked that I be given a special helper to assist me with my tapings. Finally my wish was granted with Styhe's appearance. At my request, Styhe spoke on television when WMAR, the Baltimore affiliate of NBC, filmed a special about my taping in my office.

One of the greatest rewards of my work has been to aid those who are grief-stricken with loss of a loved one, to give them hope and comfort in the knowledge that those they loved are continuing to live on the other side. We have been successful at times in "crossing the bridge" to one another. As the one left behind tells the individual that he or she is missed and still loved, and the voice from the next dimension replies *"I love you, too,"* one would have to be devoid of all compassion not to find the moment extremely moving.

The voices communicating with me run the complete gamut of human personality. Many I look upon as friends. Spirit personality is not greatly different from its human counterpart. Spirit psychology is closely aligned with human psychology. This makes it easier for meaningful contacts to take place once they are established.

What can be said of the dimensions that lie beyond the physical? Here again, I have had questions answered. The spirit voices have told me many things about time and space. They have touched upon different realities. We have gone into such matters as UFOs and reincarnation. Not all of my questions have been answered. There is still much to learn.

I have been searching since I was a child for evidence that humans survive death. It has been a long search, one that has frequently met with failure. Always hoping but never certain of success, I persevered and eventually found answers. This book is a result of my research, and the research of others, which continues today.

Chapter 2—The Background of Spirit Communications

Direct voice phenomena is not something new. Manifestations of voices from other dimensions have been occurring for thousands of years. The only difference now is that we can each do our own talking and receiving. Thirty years ago we had to go to someone "gifted," a medium, who claimed he or she could talk to those in the spirit world. With the arrival of the tape recorder, anyone who wishes can become his or her own medium.

One of the best sources for us to turn to if we wish to study early voice phenomena is the Bible, which abounds with incidents of individuals calling on God and hearing an answer. At other times a voice would speak to an individual without having been called, much as our unexpected drop-in guests speak today through the recorder.

In the New Testament an angel of God speaks to Cornelius in Chapter 10 of Acts and tells him to send his men to Joppa to bring Simon Peter back to him. When they arrive at the house where Peter is staying the Spirit speaks to Peter: "The Spirit said unto him, 'Behold, three men seek thee. Arise therefore, and get thee down, and go with them, doubting nothing, for I have sent them' " (verses 19–20).

In Corinthians Book II, Chapter 12, verses 2 through 4, Paul discussed a man he knew who was "caught up" and taken to the third heaven, where he heard "unspeakable words." He also said he knew not whether the man was "in the body, or out of the body." This is interesting, for it shows that Paul accepted astral or out-of-body experiences as well as different levels in the spirit world. Both of these topics today have their staunch supporters as well as their skeptics.

The book of Revelation by Saint John the Divine is composed entirely from what John said God's angel, as well as God directly, revealed to him.

Moving to more recent times, mediums and spiritualists have been saying all along that spirits talk to them. Because many of them have been caught innumerable times in flagrant deception, they are all frequently looked upon with a jaundiced eye. This is unfortunate, for there have been individuals who, through the years, have demonstrated genuine gifts. The taint from the dishonest mediums has clouded the whole picture of mediumship. Recently I had one medium, whom I fully trust, say to me, "Everyone thinks we're all a bunch of crooks."

Emanuel Swedenborg, born in 1688, was a Swedish scientist, philosopher, and theologian. He was a scientific genius. Among his accomplishments were discovering a method of finding terrestrial longitude by the moon, formulating a geometrical explanation of physics and chemistry, and expounding theories closely resembling those of modern physics. He was also deeply involved with physiological studies and made many discoveries that are still applicable today.

Eventually he turned to theology and said this was in response to a divine call. He stated that he could enter and be a part of the spirit world as easily as he was a part of this world and was evidently comfortable in both, frequently contacting spirits and visiting their world. Swedenborg demonstrated numerous paranormal insights that later proved to be true, so we should at least give his claims some consideration.

Swedenborg never founded a church, but in 1784, twelve years after his death, a few of his disciples began The New Jerusalem Church (better known today as the Swedenborg Church), and although it has only a small membership, branches are found throughout the world.

Eileen J. Garrett, the Moore sisters, John Sloan, Arthur Ford, and Mrs. Leonard were other mediums who seemed at times to be in touch with those who had died.

Mrs. Garrett has been quoted as saying that if someone on the earth plane is really in touch with a spirit entity, that entity should be able to give genuine information about the spirit world. Those of us who work with the electronic voice feel the information we receive from the spirit world is authentic, at least as far as the communicating spirit knows.

Another problem further clouding the authenticity of mediums' ability to communicate with the deceased is that some of the most gifted mediums are not above stooping to fraud upon occasion. If something comes through to them paranormally, they use it. If not, they create their own phenomena. Frequently it is difficult to know if certain information is genuine or not. Mediums have been castigated severely for this, and rightly so. However, the public needs to share in the blame. When a true psychic cannot come up with results consistently, often the public quickly abandons him or her and turns to those who can offer only spectacular demonstrations. Clients of psychics should be more patient and not demand that a psychic "produces" every time he or she sits down. This is a main cause of the dishonest state of mediumship.

There are two basic types of sittings or séances that mediums give during which voice manifestations occur. In the first, the medium goes into a trance, and then in a short time appears to speak in the voice of a departed spirit, usually to one of the participants in the room. This communication can last for an hour or longer. It is true that most individuals who take part in a sitting such as this are in a susceptible mood. It is very easy to believe that a voice who calls you by name and says he is a departed loved one comes from the personality he claims to be. Still, there is evidence on record of voices having said something evidential that only the person at the sitting and the spirit personality would have known. This can't all be ascribed to telepathic thought that the medium is able to pick up from those with him in the room. While a name or an isolated piece of information may be gotten telepathically, long and often complex messages are most unlikely to occur in telepathic communication. In addition, spirit voices speaking through the entranced medium sometimes give precognitive information to one of the members of the group that later proves to be correct.

The other type of sitting, which is more related to our present-day efforts in recording voices on tape, is the direct voice communication. In this, a spirit voice, independent of the medium, speaks—again usually to a participant of the séance. In the past this was accomplished most often through the medium's trumpet. At first whistles or knocks might be heard from within the trumpet, or anywhere in the room. Paranormal lights could be seen, cool breezes and gentle pats felt. The trumpet might at times become airborne, flying rapidly around the room, pausing briefly here and there in front of someone, perhaps giving him or her a light tap before whizzing on again. Such a trumpet looks like an ordinary trumpet or megaphone and is made of metal. Most have a luminous band at the wide end, which enables the people present to see it even after all the lights have been turned off. Voices would come out of the trumpet. Sometimes they would be faint and heard with difficulty, while at other times the volume would be loud enough for everyone to hear them clearly. Trumpets, although not used as frequently now, are still favored by some groups.

This is true of voices picked up on tape during recordings. Another way in which taped spirit voices are similar to direct voices, is that paranormal voices, whether speaking through the medium's trumpet or through a tape recorder, rarely have the energy to sustain themselves for any length of time.

The Ouija board, table tipping, automatic writing and music, and paranormal knocks and raps, while without voice manifestation, are some of the additional ways spirits may use to try to communicate with us. Many parapsychologists insist that it is the subconscious of the individual that activates these phenomena and not spirits. They are undoubtedly correct for the most part. There are occasions, however, when facts unknown to anyone present are given and later verified. It seems that many individuals start with that old standby, the Ouija board, obtainable in most toy stores. After they have what they feel is some success, they move on to automatic writing or even to speaking in an altered voice, which is the vehicle supposedly chosen by a spirit to communicate with our world. Some are unquestionably looking for attention from the public, others are self-deluded, and a few seem to be genuine.

Mrs. John Curran of St. Louis, along with a friend, started to use the Ouija board in the early 1900s. She soon appeared to come under the control of a girl named Patience Worth who lived in England in the eighteenth century. Patience "dictated" three novels and a number of poems, at times in an Anglo-Saxon dialect, through Mrs. Curran. This literature has become famous in the field of paranormal writing. Psychical investigators studied Mrs. Curran and all were convinced of her honesty and sincerity. They felt Mrs. Curran would have been unable to write the way she did, giving accurate details of life in the 1700s in England, unless she had received some type of paranormal help.

Some famous musicians also have seemed anxious to let us know that they have survived death. They have spoken through mediums as well as seeming to control them in the composition of new music. At times they will identify themselves, at other times not.

Some time ago, I made a survey of over two thousand individuals listed in *Who's Who.* I sent a form which requested that they describe any experience they'd had that they felt was paranormal. A number replied, telling me in detail about things that had happened to them that were unexplainable. One thing the survey showed was that the famous are just as liable to have paranormal experiences as those who are not famous.

Donald Martino, composer and chairman of the Department of Composition for the New England Conservatory of Music in Boston, who was awarded the Pulitzer prize for music in 1974 for his *Paradiso Choruses* wrote: "In my creative life I have often had the sense that my work was being 'guided.' . . . With my *Paradiso Choruses* of 1974 that feeling was so intense and so unrelenting (so near) that the term 'guided' must be replaced by 'controlled.' "

Rosemary Brown of England claims she is another who is under the control of famous musicians. Unlike Donald Martino, Mrs. Brown has not had formal musical training. Mrs. Brown worked for some time in a school kitchen in one of the poorer sections of London. From childhood she has been clairvoyant and claims that when she was seven she had a vision in which a white-haired man told her he would return to teach her music when she was an adult. In 1964, this same entity reappeared, whom she then recognized as Liszt, and began teaching her how to play the piano. Later he began to guide her hands in new compositions and soon was joined by equally famous musicians such as Chopin, Grieg, Bach, and Beethoven, all anxious to dictate new music through her.

Mrs. Brown has played some of her four hundred compositions from "beyond" over television and in concert halls. Whether they come from the purported composers has been debated by critics. Another Pulitzer prize recipient for music, the chairman of the Department of Music for a college in the East told me: "Any gifted graduate student in music could do as well." This may be true, but I think we should remember that Mrs. Brown is not a gifted graduate student and also lacks musical training. Her honesty has been thoroughly investigated, and all agree that whatever the source of her music, she must be receiving paranormal help.

One thing we need to keep in mind when we consider the claims of others who say a well-known writer, musician, or artist is communicating through them, is that the recipient of the alleged communication is like a receiving station. Those on the other side appear to be aware of who has the ability on this plane to receive what they send. Like our own electronic receivers, however, some are better than others, and even the best produce static at times. Many times the work that has supposedly come to us from "beyond the grave" is called a poor, weak imitation of the original master. This may not be the fault of the master but of the receiver, who has a tremendously difficult task under the best of conditions. In addition, the communicator may be more anxious to prove that humans survive death than to add a new number or work to his collection.

An increasing number of people today are meditating, and some are able to enter a light or deep trance state. Sometimes those who go into trance say spirit voices speak to them. Since these are all silent voices in that no one but the individual in trance can hear them, they can neither be proved nor disproved.

I conducted a series of experiments with a medium who went into a light trance, and then at the end of each experiment wrote down what he had heard the voices say. During this time, the recorder was on and we both hoped that what he'd heard while in trance would be on the tape. It wasn't, but there were other voices with messages that were pertinent to the situation.

The present phase of voice phenomena is still relatively young. In the 1950s, George Hunt Williamson, who appears to have been the first, tried to tape paranormal voices. According to his book *The Saucers Speak*, a radio engineer with whom he worked received messages in Morse code from what they felt were beings from outer space.

In 1956 Attila von Szalay of California recorded unexplained voices on tape. He was joined in his experiments by many people including psychical investigators D. Scott Rogo and Raymond Bayless. All agreed that definite paranormal voices, some very clear, were coming through the recorder. Since Szalay seems to have many mediumistic gifts, it was felt that his outstanding success was a result of these abilities.

Three years later, Friedrich Jürgenson, a Baltic painter and filmmaker, discovered he was also recording voices of unknown origin on tape. In his obituary written by W. M. Hearon, a personal friend of Jürgenson's, for *Fate* magazine (March 1988) Hearon wrote that Jürgenson had been recording bird songs and on tape playback heard a male voice clearly saying in Norwegian, *"Nocturnal bird voices."* A month later, additional messages were recorded including a woman's voice he recognized as his deceased mother, saying, *"Friedrich, you are being watched."* From then until his death in October 1987 he devoted himself to recording paranormal voices. He came to feel that they were the voices of the departed who wanted to communicate with us, to establish a "bridge" between their dimension and ours. Jürgenson wrote two books about his work published in Swedish: *Voices from the Universe* and *Radio Contact with the Dead*. When he died in his eighties, he was known as the grand old man of voice phenomena.

Konstantin Raudive, psychologist and philosopher, is the person largely responsible for bringing voice phenomena on tape to the attention of the rest of the world. He read one of Jürgenson's books and was so intrigued with the idea that he wrote and asked if he might join him for recording sessions to see what methods he used. Permission was granted, so in April and June of 1965, Raudive visited Jürgenson at his estate in Sweden. He came away convinced of Jürgenson's honesty and that spirit voices were being recorded. From then on until his death in September 1974 Raudive conducted his own experiments from his homes in Sweden and Germany. At the time of his death he had on file thousands of voices of paranormal origin.

Dr. Raudive wrote about his experiments in his book *Breakthrough*, translated into English in 1971. The book did not create the anticipated stir. Anyone who reads it will find it heavy going.

Almost three hundred pages are devoted to messages received in a foreign language and their translation into English. Dr. Raudive was an individual with whom it was evidently difficult to work at times. He was convinced, according to reports, that his interpretation of the messages was always the correct one, and in addition to this, he attributed philosophical meanings to many messages that came through, with which others could not agree. In spite of the controversy surrounding him, his accomplishments, which are numerous, deserve appreciation from all of us for the major pioneering contribution he made to the whole field of the electronic voice.

Jürgenson's and Raudive's work differs from that of the spiritualists and others who claim they are in contact with the spirit world because they helped show us, first, that voices can be recorded and, second, how it is done. Previously we had to accept the word of mediums that spirits could speak. Now we know they do, for we have the evidence on tape. We don't have to go to someone else to bring us voices from the beyond. We can do our own talking and ask our own questions about what concerns us. If we wish, we can try to contact those we have loved who are no longer here. The tape recorder has replaced the medium. It has become the intermediary between this world and the next.

Chapter 3—The Voices on Death and Dying

Death opens unknown doors. —John Masefield

With the publication in 1975 of Raymond Moody's book *Life After Life*, death, as a topic of discussion and conversation, has become less embarrassing and even acceptable. The book quickly reached the bestseller list and remained there for weeks. Moody, with his "discoveries," was looked upon by some as a prophet. Others, including Dr. Moody's publisher, Mockingbird Books of Atlanta, Georgia, had difficulty believing all that Dr. Moody had written. The editor, who had heard about the research done by Dr. Elisabeth Kübler-Ross with dying patients, sent the manuscript to her and asked if the book was accurate. She replied that it was and that in her own work had come across the identical situation time and time again. Working independently of each other Dr. Moody and Dr. Kübler-Ross had discovered the same thing.

At the Hour of Death, by Drs. Karlis Osis and Erlendur Haraldsson, published in 1977 by Avon, further explored the question of dying. The book presents the results of research on over one thousand cases the two doctors studied in comparing deathbed experiences of American and Indian patients. The two cultures being radically dissimilar, one would expect that the results obtained would be very different. This was not the case. Regardless of culture or religion, the dying patients frequently reported seeing departed friends or relatives who had come to "take them away." Sometimes they heard music or had glimpses of other worlds, which, in many cases, were described as beautiful and serene. More than once they told about entering this new world and being sent back to the earth plane, for it was not yet time for them to die.

Careful records were kept as to the type of disease or injury present, the amount of fever and the kind of drug, if any, administered to the patient. It seemed to make no difference. If anything, those who had little or no drugs in their system and were free of fever reported deathbed experiences more clearly suggestive of postmortem existence than those who were under heavy medication and had high fevers.

Dr. Kenneth Ring, a professor of psychology at the University of Connecticut, has written two recent books about the near-death experience. For the first, *Life at Death*, Dr. Ring interviewed over a hundred men and women who had come close to death. He confirmed many of the findings of Drs. Moody, Osis, and Haraldsson but discovered what he called the "core experience," which tended to unfold in a series of five stages. In his latest book, *Heading Toward Omega*, Dr. Ring continues his research into the meaning of the near-death experience.

Unknown to most people, similar studies have been made by other parapsychologists since the 1880s. Sir William Barrett, James H. Hyslop, and F.W.H. Myers, three early pioneers in the field of parapsychology, were all interested in deathbed visions and wrote about the evidence for the survival of the human personality.

It has been suggested by skeptics that the dying may only be hallucinating and seeing what they want to see. They feel that a dying person goes through severe psychological stress, and it is a comfort for this individual to see a loved one nearby, whether he or she is there or not. In many cases this may be true, but some dying patients report seeing a "fearful" figure standing by ready to bear them off. Frequently a patient is not aware that he or she is dying and still reports seeing the "take-away" person.

Even harder to explain are the "Peak in Dairen" cases. In this situation a dying individual describes seeing a deceased relative or friend whom he did not know had died. There are many of these cases on record, and in some instances the people in the room with the dying patient also did not know that the "take-away" entity had died. This must rule out the possibility of telepathic thought being picked up by those who are dying.

There is some difference between Dr. Moody's research and that of Drs. Osis and Haraldsson. In the Moody book those he interviewed had been near death or declared dead for a short time but were then resuscitated. They came back to talk about it. Most of the cases reported in *At the Hour of Death* were of dying patients describing what they saw and then going on to complete their death experience. It is noteworthy that there is a close correlation in the reports from both types of patients.

In my own work I have frequently attempted to obtain additional information to confirm or deny the discoveries others have made in the area of postmortem survival. If those I am in contact with who have already completed their death experiences report the same type of experiences as those interviewed by Drs. Moody, Osis, Haraldsson, and Ring, then the whole field of death and dying must be given further serious consideration. We can no longer dismiss the reports as the result of fevered imaginations undergoing emotional and psychological strain. Those who speak to me have died. They no longer physically exist on the earth plane but have gone through the transition known as death.

There are many enigmas in voice recordings, and one of them is that when I begin to try to explore a certain area with the other side, I am frequently put in touch with the situation itself.

An example of this is my contact with Paul. I had asked questions for several days about dying. Then, whoever it is that controls my recordings in the next dimension brought Paul and me together.

One evening early in the spring I asked if I had friends present. An unknown entity replied clearly, *"I'm Paul White."* As is my custom, I always invite someone who has given his or her name in this fashion to speak in the following recording. This is what I did with Paul, and he responded immediately in a loud, clear Class A voice, *"The light's so big. What has happened?"* Most tape recorders have digital counters that show the person taping or the listener just where he or she is on the tape while making a recording or playing one back. I carefully noted where Paul's message was heard on playback and saw that three counters later he gave a final message. He repeated the word *big*, saying, *"That's so big."*

From Paul's voice, which sounded amazed and bewildered, and especially from his message, in which he spoke about the "light," I began to suspect he had just died. The published work of others reveals the dying often report seeing a bright or white light. Paul had reported this light. In the third recording that evening I once more called on Paul and asked if there was anything further he would like to say.

He replied, *"That is the same,"* indicating the light was still there.

The following morning I was back at my tape recorder and again called upon Paul. I told him that if he had another message for me, I would like to hear from him.

Notice Paul's answer: *"That's still the same."*

For me ten hours had passed from the time Paul said, *"That is the same,"* until the next message, *"That's still the same."*

To Paul it seemed but a moment.

There is a theory, which we will explore later on, that if the spirit world exists, space and time will be different there from what we know. Paul seems to suggest this in his messages.

I was starting to become concerned about Paul. Could he be one of those individuals reported by mediums who become "caught" between the earth and spirit planes? How long does it take to make the journey between the two worlds when one is dying? This is something unknown, because at least until I had heard from Paul, I had been unable to talk to anyone who was undergoing the complete death experience. Those who come back from a partial experience seem to think everything happened quickly. Paul appeared to feel the same way, but my watch told me that almost a half day had elapsed. In addition, I still could not be entirely sure that Paul knew he had died. His voice continued to sound puzzled, and I had the impression he was starting to feel lost.

As gently as I could, I told Paul what had happened to him. I told him the light he saw was there to guide him, that he should move toward it and at the same time look for a friend or loved one who had passed on earlier and would help him into the next dimension.

That evening, twelve hours later, I again called on Paul and asked if he still saw the big light. Instead of answering me directly, Paul appeared to be talking to someone else who apparently had come to help him. He said, *"See how white it's gotten?''* The second individual replied, *"Yes."* From this I gathered that Paul was now closer to the next plane. His message indicated he was moving and no longer stationary.

This ended my personal contact with Paul. Two days later I asked about Paul and where he was. Someone answered, *"Two places are looked over."* We can interpret this to mean that Paul, as well as everyone else, has some choice as to where spirit life will begin.

What of the individual who comes to meet and help those on their way who are dying? Paul suggests this happened to him in his last message, in which he is talking to someone. Not long ago an individual told me happily, *"One great, great company greeted me."*

The guide has been described differently by various individuals. It is most often a beloved family member or close friend. Religious figures are also seen at times or "beings of light." My own work bears this out.

During the two days I was in contact with Paul I asked who the "being of light" is who meets those who are dying. Someone answered in clear, measured rhythm, *"This is one, just one."* In other words, yes, "a being of light" is one guide but there are others.

A few weeks later I asked the same question. This time someone said, *"Gracious Storm Mother. Gracious Storm. Will you help me?"* This suggests there may be a religion that calls upon a "Gracious Storm Mother" in time of need. During this same recording I asked how the person helps who comes to meet you. A female voice of unusual quality answered, *"There's nothing we shouldn't do."*

The thought held by some that those who take their own lives should be condemned to hell has always bothered me. Personally I never accepted this idea. Since I stopped believing in the traditional heaven and hell at the age of seven, the only place I thought suicides went was into the ground with everyone else. My concern was more for the memory of the poor souls who found life so desperate they felt they could not go on. To me that was hell enough.

My question as to how the death experience differs for those who commit suicide and those who pass on normally is answered in an unusually loud voice. Someone said, *"Shock!"* In an earlier recording the same morning I had asked if those who take their own lives have a bad death experience. A male voice replied, *"Yes. I have experience to death."* From the voice, which spoke slowly and sadly, and from the message itself, I had the feeling that this individual had committed suicide. My question about whether the suicide victim ever moved into the peace and comfort of the spirit world brought the reassuring answer, *"Yes. Seek out him."*

We have read about people who die but do not seem to realize that they are dead. They know something has changed. There is a difference, but they don't understand what it is. There are various reasons for this, but the major one appears to be that for many individuals the moment after death is the same as the moment before. If we are convinced consciousness will end at the time of death and it doesn't, then it isn't strange that we think we are still living even after our bodily functions have stopped. If we expect to find ourselves in front of the pearly gates of heaven with Saint Peter holding the Book of Records, and no such thing happens, it stands to reason we must think our time has not yet come. Conversely many people know they have died. They often feel lost and frightened.

Drs. Osis and Haraldsson point out in their book that not everyone who dies has a deathbed vision. Many people expire without giving any sign that they have seen a friend or loved one who has come to take them away.

My own work seems to give further evidence to what death-bed researchers have noticed. Repeatedly cries for help are recorded. *"Help me. Help me. Please help me"* has been received so often that I have lost count. It is possible some of these pleas come from those who have not had the good fortune to see someone standing by to help them at the time of death.

Occasionally after a cry for help, someone will say, *"Help here."* Then I know everything will be all right. If I don't hear these comforting words, I do what I can. After a brief prayer I suggest they look for a bright light, and if they see it, to go in that direction. I also tell them to look for a friend, a loved one, or a friendly guide who is standing by to help them.

On tape playback I may hear at the end of my remarks, *"Thank you,"* or, *"I love you."* At times someone will say, *"Help me come back."* I must then tell this individual that I can't do that. I explain that he has left his physical body and is moving on into the next dimension; that I am sure before long he will find great happiness in this new life. I close by saying that if he would like to speak to me in the future through my tape recorder I will be happy to hear from him. This has always ended our contacts with each other.

"I'm dead" has been recorded more than once. Sometimes this announcement has been followed with a request for help.

Last spring I asked my special helper, Styhe, mentioned in Chapter 1, if there are individuals who still can't believe they are continuing to live after leaving their physical bodies. He replied, *"This is right. You'll find them."*

Grief of parents who have lost a child is difficult to bear. It is interesting that children, even very young children, have death-bed experiences similar to adults. They have glimpses of happy lands. They call by name a grandparent, or aunt, or uncle who has preceded them in death, reaching out their hands to the person, smiling. Like adults, not every child wants to go. The twelve-year-old dying daughter of a friend grabbed her father and pleaded with him to hold her. "They've come for me," she said. "They don't understand I'm not ready to go."

Children have come through and spoken to me from the next dimension. They always sound happy. Frequently they are with an adult. Children's voices are usually very clear. They are high and full of vitality. I have tuned into brief conversations with children talking to adults. In one case a male voice, speaking to a child, said, *"Shout me!"* The child replied, shouting, *"All right. Boy."*

Another time a woman and a child sang their conversation to each other. It went like this:

WOMAN: *"Do you want to help me?"*
CHILD: *"All right."*
WOMAN: *"Come."*
CHILD: *"I will come!"*

The messages just mentioned, the one with the boy and man, and the child and woman, are on a thirty-minute tape I made recently for Elisabeth Kübler-Ross. The tape, *Life Beyond Life*, is intended for use by those who are terminally ill or who are having difficulty coming to terms with the death of a loved one.

My question to the voices as to what happens to children who die received the answer, *"They go in their way."*

In the following recording I asked if they meant children go in the way that has been planned for them. Two different voices replied: the first, a male voice, said, *"Like that,"* and two counters later a female voice added, *"Please tell her."*

Those who speak to me from the other side feel free to give their opinions about numerous situations that arise. More than once I have wished they would keep their thoughts to themselves, but on analysis I had to agree their comments showed an insight I lacked at the time.

I had read that a well-known parapsychologist was starting a study of deathbed experiences. I decided to send him a duplicate of the Paul White communications since they seemed pertinent to the field. Several hours were spent making a duplicate cassette tape of the contacts Paul and I had with each other and composing an accompanying letter explaining the situation and under what conditions the messages had been received. At eleven o'clock that night I told my friends on the other side what I had done and that I would mail the letter and tape the following morning.

Imagine my chagrin when I heard on tape playback, *"It won't do. Forget it!"* During the five-minute recording, not realizing someone had given this message, as I let the tape run blank for a minute, I had gone on to ask what the intended recipient of my letter would think about it. Immediately after my question someone replied, *"He just said, drop it!"*

In the following recording I asked why they didn't want me to send it. Someone replied, *"He is blind."*

The next morning, hoping to get a different opinion regarding my proposed communication with the parapsychologist, I asked the voices if they thought it would be harmful to send the tape and letter to him. Someone said in a clear voice with an echo effect, *"I told you not to."*

I was in something of a dilemma. Were my unseen contacts right or wrong? Should I send the tape and letter or destroy them? No one is infallible, in this dimension or the next, so perhaps those who told me to forget the parapsychologist were wrong. I decided to send them. A week later both were returned along with a brief note from the gentleman concerned. He wrote that he was too busy to listen to the tape. The comment received a week earlier, *"He is blind,"* seemed apropos.

An unusual recording was made one evening last summer. A

noted personality had died that day, and so during the first evening recording I asked about this person. Excited voices were heard in the background then, one voice standing out above the others saying, *"He's coming back!"* A minute or so later a high shrill voice complained, *"Let me be! I've been tied down. I've been sick!"*

Whether it was the individual I inquired about or not, I have no idea. From the messages, however, it seems as if someone may have been returning to consciousness after having reached the next plane.

The evening of May second, I received a phone call from my Aunt Jane's sister-in-law saying they had taken my aunt to the hospital in the ambulance that afternoon. Jane was no longer able to breathe without an oxygen mask, so the end was near. Jane never had children. There were no nephews, and I was the only niece, so perhaps because of this, she and I had always had a close relationship. Although we lived three hundred miles apart and, in the last ten years, saw each other just once or twice a year, letters and phone calls kept us in touch.

Five years ago it had been discovered that Jane had cancer. An operation followed and after that the usual chemotherapy treatments. For several years Jane seemed to have won her fight, but then, as so often happens, cancer was discovered again. Nine months before her death, she was back in the hospital not expected to live, but she rallied and, to everyone's amazement, returned home. Jane fought the disease. She refused to give in. When I had visited her in the hospital nine months earlier, thinking I would never see her again, she handed me a check and her driver's license renewal, asking me to mail it for her. She had renewed it for three years.

A number of people facing death deny it, not only to others but to themselves. We are told by thanatologists, those who make a study of death and dying, that we should help the dying face their death. This is important and necessary, but I think we must wait until those near death indicate they are ready. It is not a kindness to force them prematurely to look at what death means for them personally. The dying usually know subconsciously, if not consciously, what is happening. Many will give a clue to someone they love and trust that now they need and want the comfort and understanding of this other person to help them prepare for what lies ahead. We must be alert for this clue, because once given, it may not be repeated. If it never comes, then we must also accept this as a dying wish of one we love.

The denial of death can work two ways. It can and does happen that instead of offering the reassurance and support sought by the dying person, the loved one denies the reality of approaching death. This is a great tragedy and places a heavy burden on both sides.

Aunt Jane had many close friends. After her sister-in-law's husband died ten years ago, Jane continued to include Wynne as much in her social activities as she had before Bob's death. They lived in the same town, and rarely a week passed that they didn't visit or go somewhere together. Yet when Wynne called to tell me Jane had reentered the hospital, she said, "Jane still doesn't realize how bad off she is. She wore her pearls and earrings in the ambulance."

I knew differently. She had begun to accept and come to terms with approaching death shortly after leaving the hospital nine months before. It was easier for her to write about this in letters and discuss it over the telephone with me than having to look into the face of someone she loved, like Wynne, and say, "We both know I'm dying."

When Jane first said this to me in a phone call late one Sunday evening, my first impulse was to assure her she would be all right. I wanted to deny what she said, but then I didn't. Jane found comfort in being able to write and talk to me. She knew I would accept whatever she said and that she could rely on my continued love and understanding.

Jane knew about my work in the field of reincarnation, and I am sure this is one reason why she turned to me for help. Reincarnation implies survival of the human personality, and Jane wanted to be reassured about this. I never told her that my interest in survival had led me into a new area of research—that of the electronically detectable paranormal voice. My sanity, as well as morality, has been questioned at times by those who learn about what I do. Jane could accept my part in the field of reincarnation, but I was not sure she would do the same with the paranormal voice phenomena.

As death came closer Jane continued to face it courageously, but I could feel that she wanted additional reassurance from me that death would not be the end but a new beginning. It was then that I decided to share with her my contacts with the other side through a tape recorder. She accepted the news gratefully and could even begin to look forward, to a certain degree, to her new adventure. "I'll try to speak to you once I get wherever I'm going," she said. I assured her that I would be listening.

A psychiatrist would probably say that Jane had a psychological need to believe in the voices. I am sure this is true. To me, however, it is not a dreadful thing to try to answer another person's cry for help with what we can honestly say we believe in. Need or not, Jane and some of her friends have spoken to me from the next dimension.

There is a reason for everything that occurs, and I feel my involvement with Jane before and after her death was meant to be shared. Jane would be the first to say, "Let others know what has happened." The thought that she can still help from the other side those who will face a similar situation someday will bring her joy.

The evening I learned that Jane had entered the hospital, I went to my tape recorder and told those on the other side my aunt was dying. As I was talking someone broke in and clearly asked, *"Is that true?"* A second individual replied, *"That is so."* I finished the recording by requesting that my father and grandfather go to her and keep her under their love and protection. A voice said, *"This is done."*

The following evening when I asked if I had friends present, someone answered, *"This is a friend of Auntie Jane."*

The morning of May fifth, when I again asked if I had friends with me, a close, male voice told me, *"I visited with Jane."* Later that morning I asked if Jane realized they were visiting her, and the answer came back: *"Yes. She outlined."* This suggests to me that while Jane may not have seen her "visitors" clearly, she saw the outline of them.

Jane died peacefully the evening of May fifth. It was nineteen years to the day of her brother's death.

The following day, almost twenty-four hours later, I made one recording before leaving for Jane's home. I asked if she had entered the spirit world yet, and someone said, *"Yes, she did."* Six counters later there was the additional message, *"She's right here,"* and two counters after this, was heard, *"Very good now. Go ahead, speak!"* Five counters later the message, *"I'm good. I'm back here now,"* was received.

One of the effects the cancer had upon Jane was to make her

voice hoarse the last six months of her life. It was Jane's voice, still hoarse, that had told me, *"I'm back here now."* The joy I felt knowing that Jane and I could continue to speak to each other from one dimension to the next is hard to describe.

After returning from her funeral several days later, I asked if she was standing by. *"Every day"* was the reply.

The following day I received the message, *"She is still coming back."* In the next recording when I asked what they had meant by this message, someone answered, *"She's been healing."* In the third recording I asked if they meant Aunt Jane was going through healing. Two voices replied. The first one said, *"We did,"* and the second voice finished with, *"She's much better."*

Twenty-four hours later the following message was recorded: *"Stop-and-go. This is my healing, except now I'm going to rush it."*

I had to smile when I heard this. Jane was always a busy person, running here and there. Her days were never long enough, and in the years before she became ill, listening to her tell about all she had done and planned to do would exhaust me. I had a mental picture of Jane hurrying around in her new world, telling the doctors and nurses there to make her well quickly because she had a lot to do.

So Jane continues to live on another plane, in another dimension. I have heard not only from her but, unexpectedly, from a friend of hers I had met one time over thirty years ago. The two friends are together, and everything is well.

As I mentioned near the beginning of the chapter, research into near-death experiences dates back to the 1880s. Much important information has been gained from these studies, but it is only now, with the development of tape recorders, that the objective voices of the deceased can actually speak to us from the other side. They can still express love for and an awareness of those they loved and have left behind. They can, to a certain extent, tell us how things are for them in their life beyond death and something of that dimension itself. It is said that each person must die alone. From messages that have been received on tape from those who have died, I am no longer sure that this is true. Apparently many of us can hope to have the love and support of someone who has been dear and will come at the moment of death to escort us on the ultimate journey.

Chapter 4—The
Voices Tell About
the Next Dimension

"*I*t's *so pretty,*" answered an unknown friend from the other side one evening when I asked if an individual has the opportunity to go to the sort of place in the spirit world he thinks he would like. It seems that at least the person who spoke those words was where he wanted to be.

Once I became convinced that humans move on to the next dimension when they die, and survive death, I wanted to find out as much about that dimension as possible. As a result, I have asked literally thousands of questions about the dimension known as the spirit world and what life is like once we become a part of that world. I get the feeling at times that my contacts over there don't know what to do about me. For the most part, though, they seem glad for my questions and do their best to answer them. They know I want to share my knowledge with as many people as possible, and for this reason they generally accept me and my innumerable queries. I have told them that I want to be used as a channel to help our two worlds "cross the bridge" to each other, and they have replied, "*You will be.*"

There are times, however, when they are less than complimentary. This usually is a result of my persistence in asking a question they seem unwilling to answer. Last spring I had perhaps worn their patience thin by continuously inquiring if all the individuals in the spirit world can decide for themselves how to spend their time. After several days without any response, someone sounding exasperated said, *"We canvass. Stop foolish questions!"* I had a mental picture of them having a board meeting and deciding to tell me to be quiet.

More recently I had been asking about fear in the spirit world. This came about when an unknown individual, sounding very close, said clearly, *"I've got fear."* What is there to fear in the spirit world? I wanted to know. Finally someone replied, *"Stop this hounding!"*

Styhe was more tactful. Once in reply to a question he said, *"It's too soon."* From this I learned there are certain things about the next dimension they feel it is not time to disclose.

Whenever this type of message is received, I always apologize for the pressure I have been trying to place on them to answer, again explain my reason for the question, and go on to something else.

We need to keep one important fact in mind before we go any further in our discussion of what spirits say about their world, life there, and reality in general. People sometimes think once you get to the spirit world, you suddenly know everything about everything. This is not true. There are fools and knaves there, the same as here, and if you were one or the other, or both, in life, you will not suddenly go through a magical transformation as you step through death's door into the spirit world. You'll still be the same person.

Spirits do not always agree among themselves about answers to questions I ask. I have tuned in to interesting arguments one or more entities have been having. To some of my questions I have received three different answers in less than a minute.

Why bother to ask questions if the answers may be false?

Those in the next dimension are in a unique position to answer certain questions about which we can at times only try to make a more or less educated assumption. There are wise souls in the spirit world, as here, and when some of them come through repeatedly with answers, the experimenter begins to form opinions. If the same question is answered basically the same way by several entities at different times, then judgments can start to be formed. These judgments may later prove to be incorrect, but evidence can point in one direction or another.

I realize that what I say and write about the spirit world can influence some people for better or worse. It is not a responsibility I take lightly, but I would ask you to remember that those who speak through a tape recorder are still human, with human strengths and foibles. They are only a dimension away.

The following day after receiving the *"It's so pretty"* message, I asked in what way the spirit world is pretty. *"Blessing here"* was returned.

Once while I was explaining that one of my reasons for asking so many questions was to try to let others know what to expect as they move into the spirit world, someone broke in with, *"It is very, very bright."* This was said in a monotone voice in strong, measured rhythm. For a moment two voices could be heard speaking at the same time—mine and the spirit voice.

In every instance but one the answers to my question as to where the spirit world dimension is located have indicated that it is close to our own dimension. One morning in February an entity said, *"It's right on top of some."* Books on metaphysics often stress the interpenetration of the spirit world with the earth plane. This theory seems to be borne out in my own work. The one difference in opinion about the location of the spirit world came from Styhe, an individual I have come to respect for his wisdom and thoughtful answers to what I ask. He said, *"Great sum"* in reply to my question as to how far he and his friends were from me. In retrospect, I thought that Styhe may have meant this in more of a philosophical vein than in actual location.

Before proceeding, I should explain further how Styhe came to be a part of my communications with the other side. In the summer of 1977, while staying at my summer home in New Jersey, I asked one morning during my regular taping if I had friends with me. An unknown entity replied, *"This is Styhe."* I have never known anyone by that name, or even heard the name before, but there is no mistaking my interpretation of it. Unlike many other spirit voices who speak a time or two and then are not heard from again, Styhe stayed with me and has come back repeatedly. Although I have tried, I have been unable to find out anything about him and his background. My questions about how long he has been in the spirit world and where he lived while on the earth plane have all gone unanswered. He seems to feel they are unimportant, and I suppose they are, so I must accept this. I have learned that Styhe will respond only if he thinks there is good reason to do so. He will instruct me when I am seeking knowledge about life in the spirit world and, more specifically, the spirit world itself. He will not, however, answer questions he feels are only curiosity on my part.

This was brought home to me one day when I was trying to find out the name of his female associate who has also spoken to me numerous times. Styhe asked, *"Why? You are with friends."*

Those who work for any length of time with electronic voice phenomena usually come to feel they have one or more individuals on the other side who have the specific job of helping with recordings. Raudive and Jürgenson have both said that you can't record without monitors. Styhe has indicated that he is now my chief monitor, although there seem to be others working with him, such as the female already mentioned.

When I asked Styhe if space in his world was the same as in mine, if it had the same meaning to him as it did for me, he replied in an echo effect, *"Space is not the same."*

I asked what space was like. Those who speak to us seem to have their own language at times to describe something that is not a part of our language. This was one instance, for Styhe replied, *"Plata, plata."*

The next day I asked what *"plata, plata"* meant, and Styhe answered, again in an echo effect, *"It is so strange."*

During this same day I asked Styhe if space in his world has dimension like my world. He said, *"Not found like that."*

Twenty-four hours later I explored further with Styhe the question of dimension. I asked him if his world had more or less dimension than found on the earth plane. He responded, *"Your dimension is less."*

In August I returned to the question of dimension. This time I asked if one would find dimension in higher realms of consciousness. A loud, clear Class A voice answered, *"It is that bridge. The space bridge."* I puzzled over this enigmatic reply for some time and finally went back to my contacts on the other side and asked where the "space bridge" originates. In a voice still unusually clear and loud, I was told, *"The space side is you."* Although I was not prepared to give an interpretation of their message at that time, I asked if the "space bridge" is a philosophical, metaphysical type of bridge. *"That's right"* was the reply.

In recent years some mediums have spoken and written about

multiple realities and the concept that our consciousness is able
to exist on several different levels at one time. At first I dismissed these ideas as being too incomprehensible, for the
thought of them tended to make me feel disoriented. Eventually
when I permitted myself to tentatively consider the possibility
that there may be numerous realities and started to ask questions
along this line, such a flood of answers came back that I will
devote Chapters 13 and 14 to my experiments with other realities. This new vista of thought has added such depth to my work
that I feel great joy and awe at the potential that lies within each
of us.

The morning after I was told, *"The space side is you,"* I
asked if they had meant that every personality is unlimited in
its ability to continue on into many realities. *"That's right"*
was again the answer.

All of this may seem somewhat removed from my original
question about whether there was dimension in higher realms of
consciousness, but the question must have triggered the thought
in someone's mind to try to give me some new concepts of
human consciousness and its unlimited abilities. As a result of
the messages received, I am convinced that there is no latitude
or longitude in the world we will enter at death. We cannot place
the spirit world in a neat little box as many of us seem to feel
more comfortable in doing.

Those who have in the past communicated with us from the
spirit world have indicated, chiefly through mediums, that time
and dimension in their world is different from what we know.
Individuals who claim to have entered other realities such as the
spirit world through out-of-body experiences also speak about a
difference in dimension and time. One of the reasons given to
explain how those who have precognitive or retrocognitive gifts
are able to look into the future, or the past, is that for a few
moments they are able to transcend our own earth-plane limitations. The future, so they tell us, is out there ready to be looked
at, as well as the past.

Examining the theory that time as we know it does not exist
in the spirit world, I asked if there is past, present, and future
in the next dimension. The interesting answer came back in a
monotone: *"Space put on a vacuum. Nothing should be
filled."*

What did it mean? I had no idea. Perhaps I had misinterpreted the message. I gave the message back to them and asked if I had interpreted the words correctly. *"That's right"* replied the same monotone voice.

So I was back again trying to determine what was meant. All that occurred to me was that perhaps they had meant the spirit world exists in a vacuum. I had never heard this before, but having nothing else to go on, I asked if the spirit world is in a vacuum. My question didn't seem to be answered, but a voice best described as frantic said in Class A quality, *"What space doesn't?"*

This was too much for me. I dropped my questions about space for the time being so I could think over what they had said. The following morning I referred back to the message given twenty-four hours earlier: *"Space put on a vacuum. . . ."* I asked if that meant the spirit world should not be filled with dimension and time. Immediately a clear voice answered, *"Space is so much vantage."* The dictionary gives one definition for vantage point as point of view.

What those on the other side said about space over the two-day period I asked about it seems significant. But what about time in the spirit world?

Although I dropped the question of time in the next dimension, I could not forget it. Three months later I asked Styhe if they had a sense of time in his world. He replied twice, *"Yes, we do."* I asked him if they were aware of time; did it seem to move faster or slower than on the earth plane. Notice Styhe's interesting answer: He said, *"It is this, longer."*

Later that morning I asked Styhe if he meant time was longer in the spirit world because their consciousness stretches on indefinitely, while for us on the earth plane we are always faced with the knowledge that our life here must end. He replied, *"Yes,"* and four counters later added, *"Like that."*

At a later date I asked if they were able to look into the future in a precognitive way because they had few, if any, limitations of space and time in the spirit world. Someone said, *"Count of it."* Wanting to be certain of the reply, I repeated the question. This time the answer *"Is so"* was returned. Some months later I asked the question for a third time. On this occasion a voice told me that they *"looked down."* We will examine further the question of precognition in Chapter 8, but from evidential information that has been received, we must at least give serious consideration to the idea that the future is more or less already in existence.

Some of those on the other side seem unaware of my limitations. This is one of the things about voice recordings that I find puzzling. Time and again they have told me I should already know something or be able to perform certain feats of which only those in the spirit world would be capable.

An example of this happened last spring. I had asked many questions about other realities, including the reality of the spirit world, and an entity said, *"It's very different. You ought to come."*

Although it is true that some people claim to visit the spirit world through out-of-body experiences, during the only such experience I am aware of having had, I didn't go anywhere except to float around in my bedroom. I have since regretted that I wasn't more adventuresome and that I didn't travel somewhere.

I later asked how I could visit the spirit world. Several entities replied, *"Is possible. Later is possible."*

Since I like flowers, I was anxious to know if they have the same kinds of flowers in the spirit world as we do on the earth plane. *"That's right,"* a voice said.

It has always been my hope that we can continue to have pets in the spirit world. When I asked about this, the answer came back in a loud voice, *"I've had two."*

Some experimenters in the electronic voice field say they have recorded the barking of dogs that they believe to be paranormal. I have always felt that such barking came from a neighbor's dog, which the microphone picked up during a recording. This still seems to me the most likely explanation, rather than a ghostly Fido coming through on tape. It is reassuring to know, however, that it appears we won't be denied the joy of pets in the next dimension.

We are told by metaphysicians that the spirit world and those who live there operate at a higher frequency, a faster vibration than the earth plane and its inhabitants. This is the reason given for our inability to see the spirit world, which appears to exist side by side with our own world.

Last spring I asked the voices if this was accurate. An unusually clear voice replied, *"That is true."* During the same recording I asked if this was the reason we couldn't see them. Someone answered in an echo effect, *"That is it!"*

The belief that there are different levels or planes in the spirit world is acknowledged by many. Seven is usually accepted, the first being the lowest and the seventh the highest. Even Paul in the Bible, as quoted from Corinthians in Chapter 2, talked about a "third heaven." Those who hold to the belief of various planes in the spirit world usually feel that individuals are "locked" into the plane in which they find themselves at death. Through a process known as progression they can move from one plane to the next. By performing good deeds in the spirit world, or in another earth-plane life as reincarnated souls, they will be promoted to a higher level. My question as to whether it is possible to move from one plane in the spirit world to another was answered with, *"It is."*

Four days later I phrased my question somewhat differently. I asked if, as a person advances in the spirit world, he or she would go to another place. *"Moves forward"* was the reply.

When I first began recording twelve years ago, the two messages I received most frequently were, *"Help me"* and *"Cold."* While I still receive *"help me"* a moderate number of times, I seldom record *"cold"* anymore. I was not surprised at the pleas for help, but I hadn't expected to hear *"cold."* Could a person in the spirit world still have a physical feeling of cold? Upon some reflection I came to two tentative conclusions.

One explanation is that the last sensation many seem to have as they die is one of coldness. Physiologically it doesn't take long for the body to become cold and this feeling may linger even as one starts to move away from the earth plane.

Second, if there are different levels in the spirit world, one level may be damp and cold. Dante in his *Inferno* wrote that there were nine circles of hell. The ninth, and lowest, was the Lake of Ice. This is just a story, but many famous artists say their greatest works have been divinely inspired.

Moving to more recent times, Anthony Borgia wrote in a series of three books, of which *Life in the World Unseen* is one, about a low level in the spirit world that is cold and dismal. These books were the result of the purported communication between the spirit of Robert, a former Episcopal clergyman, and a friend of Borgia's, whose spirit spoke through a medium. Although I tend to have reservations about most mediumistic books, as well as those that come about as a result of automatic writing, I was interested to note that almost everything brought out in the communications from Robert was what I had previously discovered in my own work.

When I asked if in certain parts of the spirit world you might feel cold, a clear female voice replied, *"Yes,"* and two counters later, *"You write down."* Those on the other side are aware that I write all of my communications from them into a log, along with the date, time, counter on the tape recorder, and questions asked. Perhaps she wanted to make doubly sure that I had recorded her message by telling me to write it down. I next asked if I had interpreted her messages correctly, and the same female voice answered, *"You certainly did."*

While most of the people who speak to me are of the type that I am happy to call friend, there are some to whom I give short shrift. Thankfully curses and threats on my life have been few, but they have occurred. I don't invite this type of person to stay around and talk about it. Although individuals of this nature obviously need help, I doubt if anyone on this side can do much for them through a tape recorder.

Whether actual physical levels such as heaven and hell exist in the spirit world, or whether each individual creates his own heaven-hell when he gets there, much as on the earth plane, is open to debate. Many theologians would opt for heaven-hell as physical places, although a number would have difficulty accepting the "seven-plane" theory. Strangely enough, the spirits themselves don't seem sure about it.

Most of my questions about there being discrete levels in the spirit world have been answered in the affirmative. When I asked if there are dark places for those who have not lived the way they should have on the earth plane, two different voices answered. The first one said, *"That is right,"* and six counters later a second voice added, *"That's right."*

Three days after these messages were received I asked if there were higher spheres in the spirit world where "exalted" beings live. Someone replied, *"Yes, there is."*

Conversely, last summer when I asked if Swedenborg's belief, that heaven and hell are states of being and not physical places, was correct, a loud, clear voice said, *"That way."*

I then asked if a person in a state of hell and one in a state of heaven might exist side by side in the spirit world, an equally clear voice answered, *"That's right."*

What can we make of these contradictory messages from the

spirit world about heaven and hell? Are they physical places or aren't they? Why do we receive different answers from the people who should know above all, the spirits themselves?

If we look at what has been said by those who have died and then been resuscitated, we find a variety of answers. Some seem to have been in beautiful places, with green grass, lovely flowers, and friendly spirits. Others, less fortunate, report having visited dreadful realms, dank, dreary, and cold. Those spirits they met cried for help. Some appeared to be carrying heavy burdens, and others struggled on a type of treadmill.

Shortly after I began to record, I was able to get through to an older woman with whom I had had a close relationship as a child. She had died ten years previously, and yet the first time I called upon her, she responded. One of the first things I asked Elsie was where she was. *"Heaven"* was her reply. A chief aim in Elsie's life had been to go to heaven when she died, and she lived her life accordingly. It is not surprising that that is now where she feels she is.

A few weeks ago another individual told me one morning, *"We're in heaven."* I then asked this individual in what way heaven is unlike the earth plane. After a pause of about ten seconds, the same voice answered, *"I think it is nice people."*

Perhaps we can conclude from all of this that there is much more to the next dimension than anyone suspects. I have asked if mysteries remain in the spirit world and was assured that they do. This is good. As long as questions remain unanswered, we will continue to search, and in the searching, grow. Life here, as well as there, is not static.

In the end, perhaps it is unimportant whether heaven and hell are physical places or states of being. We apparently go where we belong, but like here, each individual will have the opportunity there to move on, to achieve through his or her own efforts, a greater goodness and more perfection of the human spirit.

Chapter 5—Both Sides of the Coin

> We sometimes congratulate ourselves at the moment of waking from a troubled dream; it may be so the moment after death. —Nathaniel Hawthorne

Not everyone accepts the voices as coming from other dimensions. In fact, many do not and have alternative suggestions as to what electronic voice phenomena may be. Most of the doubters admit there is something there, and some skeptics will even agree there are voices on the tapes. The origin of the voices is the question to which many address themselves so passionately. As Walter Uphoff wrote to me: "I do not think it that easy to be that dispassionate about EVP."

Many parapsychologists wish the voices would go away. They are too unscientific, too emotionally laden. These individuals, and I hasten to add this is not true of all of them, are more comfortable in their labs with their controlled conditions, trial runs, levels of significance, and so on. I don't deny that this is important research. For one thing, it has given us a more complete picture of the human personality. But I, for one, have difficulty becoming enthusiastic as to whether a person scored a level of p=.05 or .0001 in a trial run.

Parapsychologists, like the rest of us, are busy people. Too many don't have the time to get involved, to make their own experiments, or to try to find out for themselves what the voices might be. They may, I am afraid, be ready to accept the words of someone like E. Lester Smith, who in his article "The Raudive Voices—Objective or Subjective?" said he felt they had nothing to do with spirits. This first appeared in the *Journal of the Society for Psychical Research* and then was reprinted in the *Journal of the American Society for Psychical Research*. These two scholarly magazines are read by most parapsychologists, as well as others interested in the field of psychical research. Mr. Smith is entitled to his opinion, but when he writes that he has never heard tapes of the Raudive voices, one wonders just how objective he is.

Raymond Bayless, a well-known, highly respected psychical researcher and author wrote in the July 1978 issue of *Fate* magazine: "There is a modern parallel: the incredible refusal of the majority of parapsychologists to give a fair hearing to taped voice phenomena."

I have had a personal experience along this line. In the summer of 1978 I attended a conference for three days at which a notable parapsychologist spoke. On the third morning Dr. X sat down beside me in the lobby of the hotel where the conference was being held, and we began talking casually. During the course of the conversation I mentioned my work with the electronic voice. Dr. X had many questions about it, and then he said he had "great interest" in taped voices and wanted to believe in them, but as a scientist he had to be cautious, he had to be sure. I told Dr. X of my complete understanding of his position and that I felt the same way. Dr. X then said he would like to listen to the cassette tape I had brought along to the conference. We went to an empty meeting room, where I played the tape on my portable tape recorder. At the conclusion Dr. X said he was impressed, that I had the "true" electronic voice, and it was this type of voice he would like to investigate. Dr. X wondered if I would be willing to go through some tests in his laboratory with a tape recorder to see if voices could still be recorded. He complained briefly that he had never been able to find anyone who would do this. I assured him I would be more than happy to do anything at all to help prove the validity of the voices. It was my hope, I said, that the voices would become accepted by researchers such as himself, and I realized this would happen only under rigorously controlled laboratory conditions. Dr. X carefully wrote my address and phone number in his notebook and led me to believe I would be hearing from him before long.

A few days after I returned home, I mailed to him a sixty-minute duplicate cassette tape of eighty-two voices, along with a letter in which I expressed pleasure at having met him and repeated my offer to go into the laboratory under any conditions he might wish to set.

He never replied.

Why? We can only try to make an educated guess. Perhaps the answer lies in his comment the morning we met—that as a scientist he had to be cautious, he had to be sure. It could be that once he returned home and thought about it, he decided it would not be prudent to involve himself in the "gray" area of electronic voice phenomena. Many of his fellow parapsychologists would have been critical, and Dr. X may not have wanted to take the risk that his reputation might suffer under such an investigation.

I can understand his feelings even though I have difficulty sympathizing with them. His refusal to further consider the voices is typical of the parapsychological establishment as a whole. They have striven for such a long time to be accepted as a science by other scientists, many of whom still look upon them as unloved stepchildren, that they bend over backward to prove to their more "worthy" colleagues just how scientific they are. Since postmortem research is linked unfairly by many to the occult, most parapsychologists won't touch it. This is unfortunate, because in trying to prove that the human personality is capable of much more than is generally thought, they are hesitant to openly investigate the most important area of the personality's survival after death.

The "Luxembourg" effect, meaning that the tape recorder is picking up voices originating from radio or TV broadcasts when no radio or TV is on, is one way voices manifest, according to those who doubt they come from the spirit world. If this does happen one time out of a thousand, what about the other nine hundred and ninety-nine times? The "Luxembourg" effect is so rare, I think it can be dismissed as a serious consideration for the cause of the voices.

The proliferation of CB (citizens band) operators on the scene makes it more likely that their voices will be picked up by a tape recorder rather than a distant radio or TV studio. If I hear "Pretty Daisy, Pretty Daisy," or "Ten-four, good buddy" on my tape, I am not inclined to think it is a spirit.

Some people think atmospheric sounds are the culprit. They feel nothing is ever lost, including all the words we speak.

Whether they are right or wrong we won't go into here, but even granting that their premise is correct, I can't conceive how the words needed to answer the many questions I and others ask manage to come back at the appropriate moment in response.

There are skeptics who claim there aren't any voices at all on the tapes. It is only the imagination of the experimenter and mass hypnosis or telepathy of those who are called in to listen. While it is true that many who tape voices hear all kinds of marvelous things that no one else can hear, which must certainly raise the question of self-delusion, this cannot begin to explain the whole story. In the Rorschach medley of sounds, one can hear almost anything one has in mind to hear. However, there have been countless experiments in which others have listened to EVP tapes and have come to the same conclusion about various messages as the experimenter. At times the experimenter has not been near these "listen-ins," and was not even aware they were being done. In addition, these taped voices often register on sensitive oscilloscopes, and they come through on speech printers. Since such equipment does not lend itself to the hypnosis or telepathic factors, I think such hypotheses can be discarded.

How about extraterrestrials? George Hunt Williamson, in the 1950s, may have been the first to suggest the voices were coming from somewhere out in space, but he hasn't been the last.

Raymond Cass, of Bridlington, Yorkshire, England, is a British experimenter who has been successful in recording many loud, clear voices. Susy Smith mentions in her book *Voices of the Dead?* that some of Mr. Cass's tapes are being studied by colleges and research foundations in this country and abroad. Mr. Cass receives sentences at times in English and German. Since he not only understands but speaks German fluently, translation of these polyglot sentences is not a problem for him. He sent me one of his tapes, and at one point a voice came through and says they are of the *"Cosmos."* This could be interpreted to mean that the speaker was extraterrestrial or a spirit indicating that his world, the next dimension, and our world were one.

In the book *The Unobstructed Universe*, by Stewart Edward White, this is suggested by his wife, Betty, who, having passed over to the spirit world, dictated the book through a friend. While I mentioned reservations about such books previously, I feel this is one that is worthy of consideration. Throughout *The Unobstructed Universe*, Betty stresses there is only one universe, and consciousness is the only reality.

One evening a friend who also taped voices recorded, *"Hi from Jupiter!"* We discussed whether it was possibly someone from that planet or a mischievous spirit having a bit of fun. The timbre of the voice was slightly different from most of the other voices. It was more mechanical and it sounded robotlike.

Uri Geller, the controversial Israeli psychic, has reportedly had extended contact with and received many messages from the unseen through his tape recorder. In his book *Uri Geller: My Story* Mr. Geller writes that the voices tell him that they speak from a spacecraft named *Spectra*, and they have come to this planet from a planet thousands of light-years away. They give different reasons for coming, but basically they want to help us work for world peace and to keep us from destroying ourselves. Unfortunately once these messages are received they either erase themselves mysteriously or they dematerialize. This may sound incredible but others also claim to have heard the messages and were present and saw the tapes self-destruct.

As a result of my own experiences, which will be detailed later, I feel there are entities in many different realities that are capable of communicating with us in various ways. One of these ways is through a tape recorder. It is not beyond the realm of possibility that Geller's communicants are who they claim to be. If we can accept that this may happen, then we must consider what evidence there is that other EVP tapers are also recording messages from realities not commonly thought of as spirit. The idea need not frighten. All the messages I have heard on my own tapes, as well as those received by other researchers, that appear to come from nonhuman entities have given no hint that we are in danger from them. They have never, to my knowledge, threatened anyone personally on tape. There are many theories about UFOs. A large number of people accept that there is "something" flying around in our skies at times. If some of them are from other worlds, might we not also consider the idea they are not only capable but want to speak to us through tape recorders?

The most popular theory accepted by those who reject the voices as coming from another dimension is that the experimenter is having a psychokinetic effect on the tape. Psychokinesis, the ability of the mind to affect matter, has been proven under controlled conditions in the laboratory. If the voices result from the taper's brain sending out impulses, then this must be a more common ability than previously thought.

Peter Bander, a Britisher and the original publisher of Raudive's book *Breakthrough*, which he had translated into English, wrote in his own book, *Carry On Talking*, published in this country under the title *Voices from the Tapes*: "The chances against a series of electronic impulses from the subconscious manifesting themselves in sounds which correspond even remotely to common speech in any language are mathematically so great and improbable that they must be ruled out."

I have done several recordings during which, instead of recording at the usual speed of $3\frac{3}{4}$, I recorded at $7\frac{1}{2}$, which is twice as fast. On playback I switch back to $3\frac{3}{4}$. My voice sounds like a verbal version of a slow-motion movie. The words are still barely understandable, but the voice itself becomes bass, and I sound as if I am trying to talk with a mouth full of mush. It stands to reason that any other voices recorded at these times, spirit or not, should sound like mine, greatly distorted. But no! They sound like they always do. It makes no difference for them at what speed I have taped. My or anyone's subconscious would certainly be unable to compensate for the change in recording speeds between recording and playback. I don't know how the spirits do it, but I am sure such abilities lie beyond human capabilities.

Further considering whether the experimenter is able to place his voice on tape through PK (psychokinesis), Dr. John Beloff wrote an article "Voluntary Movement, Biofeedback Control and PK" that appeared in the July–August 1979 issue of *Parapsychology Review*. In it, Dr. Beloff wrote: "It may be doubted whether we can rightly speak of 'willing' in connection with PK. At most the subject can wish for a certain result to come about, but there is not much he can then specifically do to make it come about."

One of the "proofs" individuals have used to disavow the psychokinetic theory is that the person making the tape can walk out of the recording room and still pick up voices on the tape recorder left behind. These same individuals also ask how we can blame psychokinesis for the voices if the experimenter isn't near the tape recorder. I have made a number of recordings when I was in a distant part of the house, out in the yard, even driving to the bus stop, and the recorder was recording in my office. On playback there are frequently voices, sometimes Class A, and on a few occasions I've heard a conversation between two or more voices, which, because of their content, I am convinced came from another dimension.

Even with these experiences I am not sure that I can agree completely with those who say that psychokinesis doesn't play any part in voice recordings.

In the last few months my friends on the other side have been kind enough to answer some of my repeated questions about just how they are able to speak to us. The puzzle pieces are falling into place, and the picture is beginning to take form. They use our magnetism, our psychic energy, which everyone has, to help them in their voice manifestations. Even when we leave the recording room, this energy remains to a certain extent, and can be used by those spirits who try to speak to us.

There is too much evidence against voice phenomena being a strictly psychokinetic effect of the experimenter on the tape, however. For one thing, nonsense words are occasionally recorded. While I don't doubt I may have a certain amount of nonsense spinning around in my subconscious, I doubt that it would come out in Class A words such as *"roberabear," "chippack,"* or *"key-wacka."*

One evening a friend recorded a man's voice with a pronounced lisp to it. The friend has no speech impediment.

Some experimenters receive messages in a language unknown to them. As I mentioned earlier, I have received both German and French. Some of these messages made sense once I was able to translate them. I have grave doubts that unknown knowledge of foreign languages is a part of the subconscious.

I have made recordings during which I called upon Dr. Raudive. A deep male voice at times replied. I asked Dr. Raudive upon occasion to speak German as a further means of identification. He obliged. Later I was able to find some of the words in my German dictionary. He had given answers to my questions.

There have also been several instances in which a voice began to speak, realized I was still talking, stopped to allow me to finish, and then repeated what he started to say, going on to complete his own answer.

Four months after I began to record, I asked those on the other side to tell me if there was someone in charge of their world, and, if so, to tell me who it was.

The answer began as I said "world." Two words in a low male voice replied, *"There is."* This answer stopped as soon as the entity realized I hadn't finished. When I ended with "who it is" the same voice came back with *"There is the Christ."*

No matter how wonderful the subconscious is, it is not capable of such feats.

A number of years ago I began taping a number of messages telling me I should get a mirror to use with my work. I ignored the messages, for they seemed ridiculous, and certainly never mentioned them to anyone. The voices became insistent about the matter, saying, *"Get a mirror!" "I told you to get a mirror." "Talk into a mirror,"* and so on. Finally, more to quiet them than anything else, I bought a cheap mirror and placed it on top of my tape deck. The first time I used it a number of messages came through indicating how pleased they were to have it. A Class A voice said, *"If you use this mode, we can help you."*

Several weeks later, Dan McKee, a taper from Illinois called and said, "Sarah, I've been getting a lot of messages about mirrors." I then told him about my mirror messages.

Less than a month after this Mercedes Shepanek of Virginia called and said, "I've been taping mirror messages lately." I told her that Dan (whom she did not know at the time) and I had been getting the same thing.

Unique messages, such as the mirror messages, know no boundaries. Alexander MacRae of Skye, Scotland, is an engineer and one of the directors of Skyetech which manufactures products mainly in the area of speech recognition and synthesis, robotics and health goods. Before returning home to Scotland he lived in the United States for a time and worked on the staff of Stanford Research and also for NASA. He helped develop the communication system used on our first manned space vehicles. MacRae is regarded as one of the top five men in the Western world in the field of voice analysis and research. Since going back to Skye, he has become interested in electronic voice phenomena and done research in the field. MacRae is convinced we are communicating with other dimensions and has taped many paranormal voices. We have corresponded and in one of my letters to him, I mentioned the mirror messages that had been received. MacRae commented on a cassette tape, that was sent to many individuals around the world, that he *also* had received mirror messages. Like the rest of us, he was told to talk into a mirror.

These messages are reminiscent of the cross-correspondence cases famous in mediumistic literature. Four of us were taping messages concerning mirrors at about the same time with none of us realizing that anyone else was receiving similar messages.

Thus far in looking at both sides of the coin, we have dwelt mainly on what could be called technical reasons for the plausibility or implausibility of paranormal voices speaking through tape recorders. There is another area, more subtle, on the flip side of the coin at which we should also look. Morally, do we violate biblical or spiritual laws by asking spirits to communicate with us? Individuals have quoted passages from the Bible to me trying to prove that I am doing the devil's work.

Last winter I wrote to a professor at the Naval Academy in Annapolis who I felt, because of his background in sound waves, might have some valuable ideas in helping the voice to manifest on tape. In his answering letter Dr. Z first wrote that he had questions whether it was technically feasible for us to communicate with the next dimension, and then went on to say that the possibility that I might be in contact with the spirit world could not be excluded. If such was the case, he wanted to advise me to use "extreme caution," saying there are scriptural admonitions against delving into this area. He closed his letter by quoting three passages from the Bible to prove his point, and invited me to attend his church.

He is correct; there are such warnings, but we can also find passages in the Bible that support spirit-human contact. It is fortunate for us that in biblical times being in touch with spirits was not thought to be wrong. If it had been, a large portion of the Bible would never have been written. The problem with quoting isolated passages from the Bible is that one can prove—or disprove—almost anything one wishes.

Where the Bible condemns the paranormal, upon careful study, it seems to be more in relation to fraudulent practices that existed in Canaan thousands of years ago. If we read all of the relevant biblical passages there is one conclusion—that whatever our God-given talents are, they should be used to promote His kingdom here and above.

It is interesting that the first entity to speak to me above a whisper was a former minister in a church I attended some years ago. For over two months all of the messages that came through were whispered: some were loud, but still whispers. Then, one morning, this individual spoke his name clearly, although I had not called upon him. He was a dear man loved by all. One time when I asked him to try to give me evidence I was actually hearing from him he replied, *"Go in peace,"* which is the way he concluded each church service.

The Church has nothing to fear from the paranormal, for, properly used, it can be a powerful ally. Many religions assume that another reality, besides the one we know, exists. They accept the possibility of miracles, such as healing in a terminal case. Survival from death is taught in most faiths. All these beliefs are reinforced by psychical study as a whole, and more specifically by the voices that speak on tape.

The personality of the taper seems to influence the sort of message and even the kind of spirit who comes to speak most of the time. We like to associate with those who have similar feelings and ideas. Spirits are no exception. There seems to be some selection on their part as to whom they decide to speak to on this side. There are more than enough to go around for all who wish to communicate. The experimenter, however, must always use his or her own good judgment in deciding whether to respond to, or act upon, a suggestion from the other side.

In Corinthians, Book I, Chapter 12, verses 7 through 11, we read: "But the manifestation of the Spirit is given to every man to profit withal. For to one is given by the Spirit the word of wisdom; to another the word of knowledge by the same Spirit; to another faith by the same Spirit; to another the gifts of healing by the same Spirit; to another the working of miracles; to another prophecy; to another divers kinds of tongues; to another interpretation of tongues: But to all of these worketh that one and the selfsame Spirit, dividing to every man severally as he will."

As Corinthians tells us, we each have received gifts from God. It is up to each person to decide how they should be used. The tape recording of voices from beyond could be looked upon as such a gift. It is a gift I try not to misuse.

Chapter 6—The Voices Tell About Their Lives

> The tomb is not an endless night—
> It is a thoroughfare, a way
> That closes in a soft twilight
> And opens in eternal day.
> —Anonymous

When I was a child, before I decided that the tomb was the final end for everyone, I was not sure I wanted to go to heaven. Flying around, strumming harps, and singing songs all day was not my idea of fun. My fears have been allayed. From what has been received on tape the last twelve years, I know that life in the world beyond is a busy one. There is little time for choir practice.

One idea that has been advanced by certain researchers in the field of postmortem existence is that if any part of the human personality survives death, it must continue in a kind of dream state. One time I asked if existence in the spirit world was similar to our dream state here on earth. A clear, loud, monotone voice replied, *"Quite different,"* and one counter later the same voice added, *"That is so different."*

The following day I referred back to these two messages and asked what life in the spirit world was like. The interesting answer, still in the same clear monotone, was, *"This is why impediment people are instructed for that."*

By now it must be apparent that those who speak to us use unusual words and grammar at times when speaking.

Why the unexpected words and the improper grammar? If telepathy is used more than spoken language in the spirit world,

48

correct grammar could become rusty, and so when they try to get through verbally to someone on this side mistakes occur. Since they have told us that they operate at a different frequency and vibration than we do, this may also apply to their language, some speech sounds coming through more easily.

If other realities in addition to the spirit world reality are speaking to us, this could help explain the unique use of words and sentence construction. They are strangers in a strange world trying to communicate. I have been told frequently that they come to *"work"* with me, and perhaps language development is one area in which they are working.

The message, *"This is why impediment people are instructed for that,"* seems to show clearly that because of an individual's lack of knowledge about the spirit world he or she must be "instructed" in what it is like. There is good evidence from the tapes that a person is told about life in the spirit world once he or she gets there. The job would be easier for spirits, if when one dies one already knows what to expect. A minimum of time spent in instructing the person before he or she moves on to assume an active, responsible role in spirit world life would free the greeting, teaching spirits to spend their time where it is more needed.

I have noticed that when a large number of people die at one time, such as the crash of the two 747 jumbo jets in the Canary Islands in which close to six hundred people lost their lives, I record so many cries for help, I lose count. The calls in that case, incidentally, began coming through almost as soon as the crash happened, but twelve hours before I knew anything about it. After three days they abruptly stopped. It is difficult to escape the conclusion that it seemed to take that long before the spirits were able to get around to everyone there and to help them all move on into the spirit world.

Mercedes Shepanek of Virginia, who before her death in 1986 recorded voices from other dimensions through her tape recorder, had a similar experience on January 14, 1982, the day following the crash of an Air Florida plane into the Potomac River. She asked if those on the other side were aware of the crash and immediately received a number of replies. I have listened to the recording and found it extremely moving. There are many voices speaking in an excited babble. Some entities seemed confused and gave the impression that they had just died. At the same time there were other, calmer voices, who by their messages indicated they wanted to help. The first message was, "*. . . on that airliner . . .*" A moment later someone said, "*We got a loser.*" Then, "*Will you help them out?*" An entity pleaded, "*Redeem.*" This was followed at once with, "*Will you come with me now; will you come?*" Next was heard, "*I'll do it right away . . . right in the snow.*" After that came, "*Reach down . . . now reach down. . . . I don't want 'em all killed.*"

From the nature of the messages it seems evident that Mercedes was tuned in to what was happening to some of the victims of the crash.

Upon different occasions I have asked what the greatest difference is between life in the spirit world and life on the earth plane. One time a voice said, "*We have everything.*"

Ten days later I asked if a person in the spirit world has the opportunity to continue to pursue the same interests he or she had while on the earth plane, such as music, art, and writing. My question was answered with "*Yes, Estep.*"

This answer is reinforcement for what mediums have said they receive in trance from discarnate spirits. These spirits speak with evident satisfaction about being able to continue pursuing and learning more about their earth-plane interests after they move into the spirit world.

There is additional evidence that the "*Yes, Estep*" message is a valid one. In the spring when I asked if Brahms, Beethoven, Bach, and Chopin were continuing to compose and play beautiful music in the spirit world, I recorded, "*They're still playing music to share with their brothers.*"

During an early morning recording I asked if there were churches to attend in the spirit world. A powerful monotone voice answered in a strong rhythm: "*Mine. Yes, yes, for my own people.*" This reply was a surprise. I had thought that surely in the spirit world a true ecumenical feeling would prevail. It seems, at least for this individual who answered, such is not the case for him or his people.

Later in the same recording I asked if they continued to worship God in the spirit world. "*Some do*" was the answer.

In the next recording I asked if there was more than one denomination, one Church, in the spirit world. A voice said clearly, "*One choice for you.*"

Four months later I asked them to try to bring back the individual who had said he had a church for his own people. Someone said, *"Yes, he's come."*

I asked if everyone in the spirit world belonged to a church. The answer, *"Not. They can,"* is recorded. I then asked if they meant that while not everyone in the spirit world belonged to a church, they could if they wished. An easily understood, deliberate voice replied, *"This is so."*

Otto, an unknown entity, has spoken to me upon several occasions. He has a loud, clear voice and usually announces his presence with *"Otto here."* I asked him once if he was happy in the spirit world. He seemed to use unusual background audio sounds to help him speak as he said in a strong voice, *"Joyous with my friend. Happy."*

Eleven days later I further explored the question of a spirit being reunited in the spirit world with friends and loved ones known on the earth plane. Someone said, *"You can."* I asked if family relationships continue in the spirit world. *"Yes, if you let it"* was taped.

Spirits have indicated, through mediumistic communication, that loving, close relationships that existed on the earth plane can be continued in the spirit world. Where the relationship was less than ideal, you need have nothing further to do with that person in the afterlife.

One day, and not in relation to anything I had asked, someone said, *"Yes. We begin to live."* I asked if they have a fuller, more abundant life in the spirit world than on the earth plane. This time a voice replied, *"Awfully free."*

We are told by spirits, communicating through mediums, that in the spirit world we must continue working on personal growth in order to progress to a higher level. When I asked Styhe if an individual continues to work on his development from the point he was at upon leaving the earth plane, Styhe answered, *"That he can."*

In April I had been told by James, with whom I have had extended contact, that he had *"experienced hate."* Two days later I asked why individuals must continue to work on feelings of hate in the spirit world. *"You're nothing then"* was received.

In the next recording I asked whether they had meant if a person didn't continue working on this feeling of hate, he wouldn't continue to advance. Someone assured me, *"I did."*

This suggests that more value is placed on moral development in the spirit world than is often found in our materialistic earth-plane society.

When I asked what spirits continued to hate in the spirit world, someone answered, *"The wrong thing."*

About this time I asked how they solved problems in the next dimension. The sensible but not too revealing answer came back, *"Work on them."* In the next recording I asked what the greatest problem in the spirit world was, and this time a voice said, *"You find only to do good."* This somehow doesn't seem like a problem, but since the answer was clear enough perhaps it was my question that hadn't been understood. I get the feeling at times that I am a bit out of step with some of those who speak.

The subject of food seems to occupy the thoughts of some spirits. One morning when I asked who was with me, a voice replied in a slow, sad monotone, *"I sure I have not food."* Three months later, again in answer to my question as to who was here, I was told, *"Right! I don't have enough food."*

Is there food or not? Some spirits say yes, some say no. The majority don't seem overly concerned about it, as if it has lost importance. One medium told me there was no food as we know it, but a delicious kind of fruit. In one of Anthony Borgia's books mentioned in Chapter 4 his friend Robert mentions fruit in the spirit world that is unknown to us here. I have asked about this several times and once seemed to receive a faint *"Yes."*

The question of houses has caused less controversy than food. When spirits are asked about houses through mediumistic communication, the reply has always been positive. While my questions to those with whom I am in contact have brought an interesting variety of answers, all have reinforced the idea that there are houses in the spirit world.

Spirit personality has never been a subject of serious study by those researchers willing to admit the possibility of post-mortem survival. Yet, more and more is being learned indirectly, and I think anyone "brave" enough to embark upon such a project would find it a fascinating one and helpful to the rest of us. If we have some grasp of spirit personality psychology before we ourselves move on to the world beyond, our own adjustment will be less difficult. Knowledge for its own sake is important, and learning what changes the human personality undergoes at death is a worthwhile study in itself.

The answers to my questions about houses have shown subtle differences in spirit personality. Some have taken my questions literally and have given a literal answer. Others, evidently interpreting the questions to be philosophical, have given philosophical answers.

I have always made it a practice to use the language and thoughts coming to me from the other side in my return communications with them. For example, one female voice told me a few months ago to *"take a portrait"* of her with my camera. From then on, I have always referred, when talking to this person, to "portrait"-taking with my camera. So it is in the matter of houses, or anything else. If an individual shows a proclivity for looking at something philosophically, I do the same. If he or she is a nuts-and-bolts type of person, then I am also. This may be one reason why I have such a wide variety of spirits who come to talk to me through my tape recorder.

Every so often I turn the microphone over to any spirits who are present and would like to give a message. Many interesting and unexpected things have been recorded in this way. In May, during an evening recording, I invited whoever was present who wanted to speak to do so. On tape playback someone said in clear, slow, measured rhythm, *"I do want to go home."*

The following morning I asked if they had homes in the spirit world. A voice replied, *"That is very plain,"* and four counters later added, *"That is right."*

Twenty-four hours later, trying to get a more specific answer, I asked if the homes in the spirit world were much like our earthplane homes. A distinct male voice said, *"We have."*

Frequently when I show an interest in a particular area, those on the other side will go beyond my questions and give me unexpected insights and knowledge. When I stop recording, I always allow the tape to run an extra thirty seconds or so, for I have discovered that one or two last messages may come during this time. This happened during the time I was exploring the question of homes in the next dimension. I had signed off for the morning when a clear voice came in with, *"One day you're going to have to leave. One day you'll go home, I know."*

Upon consideration the implication of this message is startling.

They tell me I am going to have to leave (die) one day, and when I do, I'll go home.

Home? Where? The earth is our home—or isn't it? You remember earlier Aunt Jane said, *"I'm good. I'm back here now."*

From these messages I knew I would have to try to explore the question of home further. What they were saying suggested much more to me than a house with four walls and a roof.

The following morning when I asked the voices if they regarded the spirit world as their real home the answer *"Yes"* was returned.

On the morning of May twentieth someone said, *"We come back here."*

The next day I asked if they regard the spirit world as home, how then do they look upon the earth plane. The unexpected answer *"Death"* came back in a loud, clear voice.

Later that same morning I asked if spirits feel the earth plane is death, why do they come here. I was told, *"You should know."*

One evening in June, James said excitedly, *"I can prove."* While the first three words are clear, I was not sure about the last. The following morning when I asked James to please tell me again what he could prove, he answered, *"Second home."*

In August, when I asked Styhe if he was with me, he replied, *"Yes. That's why I didn't report to home."*

In my questions about home and life in the spirit world, I learned much more than I had expected. Chapter 9 takes a look at what spirits say about reincarnation; however, it seems to me we have some strong evidence here to suggest that the essence of each person does reincarnate. This is even stronger when we consider that in all of the spirit voices' remarks about going back home to the spirit world, reincarnation, as such, was not mentioned by them or me. What they said was unconscious evidence, and by it, they revealed through implication that humans do return, to them, home in the world beyond; to us, life on the earth plane.

One's job is important to a person, and so I have tried to find out about jobs in the spirit world. It appears we won't spend our lives in idleness there. While it won't be all work and no play, I suspect, from what has come through on tape, that we will all have the job that suits us best, not only performance-wise, but psychologically.

Some months ago, when I first began asking about jobs in the spirit world, someone said, *"We do not sleep."* I feel this was more of a philosophical than a literal answer, indicating that spirits have busy, productive lives.

In May, when Aunt Jane gave the message about her healing, I asked if there were doctors and nurses in the spirit world to help those in need of healing. Two answers came back, about a minute apart. They were *"You are seeking"* and *"That is right."*

Five weeks later, when I called on Jane to see how things were going for her, her friend whom I'd met over thirty years earlier responded. This was a surprise, for I had not given him a thought, much less called on him. I greeted him with pleasure for, to me, it was additional evidence I was getting through to Jane. Twenty-four hours later I asked if he was with me. He replied happily, *"Back again!"* When I asked what his job in the spirit world was, he answered, *"I have a nice job."* This isn't very revealing, but perhaps he thought it would be too difficult to explain because of technical difficulties, either with the recording or the job itself.

There may be a need for doctors and nurses in the spirit world besides their role in helping new arrivals. Unlike all other spirit communications I have heard about, where illness seems to be unknown, my communicators have told me that spirits can continue to feel sick at times. This seems to be more of a general condition of malaise than a specific disease.

In March, when I was calling on Styhe a number of times each day with questions about space and time, he finally told me, speaking slowly in a voice that sounded tired, *"Okay, I weak."* It was not until then that I realized spirits could have sensations of weakness. I had to, at the same time, accept the possibility that I was the cause of Styhe's weakness due to my incessant calling on him.

My question about whether spirits are weakened by being called upon frequently by those on the earth plane was answered with, *"It does weaken."*

After this I stopped calling on Styhe for two weeks so he would have the opportunity to regain his strength. When I next called on him and asked if he felt stronger, he replied in his usual clear voice, *"I feel much better now for you."*

Since then I have been careful not to call upon Styhe or anyone else excessively.

Apparently, as exemplified in the Potomac River airplane

crash, some spirits have the job of meeting new spirits at the time of death and helping them into the spirit world. What else have we learned about the work life of spirits?

As was mentioned at the beginning of this chapter, Beethoven and other musical greats seem to still be composing and playing music to *"share with their brothers."* I asked if they have pianos and piano music in the spirit world. *"We certainly do. We play"* was the Class A reply.

There are also teachers in the spirit world. This has been made clear to me more than once.

After I signed off one evening in late June, a final message came through in slow rhythm. Someone said, *"This group will be brought down to see it."* The following morning I asked if they meant they were going to bring a group down to my office to watch me record. The same voice I had heard the evening before replied, *"That's a true thought!"*

The idea was startling. Besides giving me the feeling that my office and I are on the "tour circuit" for those in the spirit world, I have a mental picture of a tour guide organizing groups of spirits to come down and watch me at work. This is not as strange as it may seem. Three mornings earlier I had taped the message, *"Good morning. Estep's rolling."*

Over the months the spirits' reason for these apparently "escorted" trips to my office became evident.

We can go out to the golf course and start swinging at a ball with a club; or we can take lessons and learn the proper approach. So it seems to be with those who speak from the next dimension. Some choose the former way, others the latter. While I am happy to hear from either type, I feel a special responsibility for those who take the time to come and try to learn more about spirit-human communication.

One evening someone, evidently the teacher, said to another spirit, *"Go ahead, talk. Be careful with her."*

The next morning, when I asked why they felt they had to be careful with me, the voice heard the evening before said, *"We will talk to her better."*

A month later, when I invited the other side to join me in my office either to speak or to just sit and observe, someone said clearly, *"We will start with that."*

From messages recorded lately, it is hard to escape the conclusion that more and more spirits are joining me in my office either to watch or to take part in the recordings, and many times someone appears to be in charge of these groups. My question about whether they have teachers instructing those who wish to speak to us was answered with, *"Right! That's right."*

One job that is evidently taken on by a certain group is the actual control of tapings. Recently a loud Class A voice said, *"Work out with Sarah."* Ten days later an equally loud voice, evidently speaking to others, said, *"Let's delay. Talk to Sarah now."* Another time two different voices spoke on the tape. The first said, *"I came here."* The second voice broke in with, *"Once again,"* and then the first entity finished the message by saying, *"We came to work here."*

Last summer I asked Styhe how it was decided where a spirit should begin spirit life. He replied, *"We sit with him."* I next asked if he had meant by this message that spirits sit and talk over with the new spirit where and in what capacity he would like to begin his spirit life. *"Yes"* was the reply.

Two days later I asked Styhe if a spirit has the opportunity to visit several places before deciding where to begin life in the spirit world. He said, *"Yes. Many places."* During this same recording I asked how one place differed from another in the spirit world. Styhe replied, *"A lot."* You may recall that when I asked about Paul White and whether he had moved on into the spirit world the answer *"Two places are looked over"* was received. These two responses about places seem to concur and reinforce each other.

Some people believe that if a spirit wants something, all that is necessary is to think about it. Thoughts can literally create, whether it be houses, flowers, or pianos. I have always found this idea difficult to accept, too good to be true. Many of my questions along this line have gone unanswered; however, a few of them have brought a response.

In January I asked if spirits could create things in the spirit world with their thoughts. The answer came back, *"Yes, it is. Yes, it is an assumption."* The second part of the response is even more interesting than the first. Are the spirits saying that they *can* create with thoughts, or by the word *"assumption"* are they referring to the belief of many on the earth plane, that spirits can think whatever they want into existence?

Two months later I asked the same question again. This answer, even more puzzling than the first, was, *"This is praydorus, we think. Yes, we do."*

The word *"praydorus"* was strange to me. I was unable to locate it in my dictionary, and then it occurred to me they might have been speaking about Michael Praetorius, a German musician of the late 1500s to early 1600s. The following morning I asked about this, and a clear, fast monotone voice said, *"I'll not disclose him. Thank you, close him."*

So I still don't know if thoughts can create objects in the spirit world, but in another area, thoughts seem capable of a good deal more there than here on the earth plane.

Most of us have some limited talent with telepathy, and a few unusually gifted people seem to be able to "read" another individual's every thought.

Thus is it with spirits: Some are more gifted than others. I have been startled more than once when they have commented about an unspoken feeling I have had concerning different situations.

Some time ago I asked if it was a correct idea that when we think about them, they are aware of our thoughts. A voice replied, *"It is divine scheme this."*

My constant contacts with those in the spirit world indicate that life there is well ordered. There is personal freedom, with each spirit carrying out those tasks for which he or she is best suited. One of the greatest surprises is that, despite the dissimilarities between our two worlds, the differences appear not as great as might be expected: It is like the earth plane, only more so, and as here, it is up to each individual to make the most of life.

Chapter 7—So
Experiments

To see if voices would come through on other occasions than my specific daily recording times, I decided to try some experiments using different people and locations.

I have usually looked upon the séances that I have read or heard about with a jaundiced eye. A ghostly figure floating around the room, a soft hand patting Uncle Ed's fevered brow, and a spectral voice assuring Sister Sue that everything is fine and dandy in the great beyond has always struck me as too likely a case of chicanery. At the same time I felt it unfair to dismiss all of them as fraudulent. Even if some sort of genuine spirit manifestation only took place one time out of a hundred, it was worthwhile investigating them further. I was especially interested in seeing if voices would speak on tape during a séance. The only way I could be sure trickery was not involved was to hold my own séance. I would choose the medium, and friends about whom I had no doubts.

One midwinter evening, Teena Johnston, who acted as medium, the six friends I had chosen, and I gathered around a long narrow table in my office. For everyone but Mrs. Johnston, this was our first séance. We were urged to watch for soft lights, to be aware of cool breezes, or anything else that might be out of the ordinary. Mrs. Johnston started calling on any spirits present to let us know they were there. Earlier that day while I was

do that evening and
ak through the tape

hour, produced no
spirit visitors except
rough the table. On
Many voices! While
loud enough to be
eard without head-

me here." At one
table vibrating. Sé-
o I answered, "I'm
"Yes, you do!" on
tape. Mrs. Johnston implored the spirits, time and again, to lift the table to show us they were present. As she was saying "Please lift the table; lift the table, please," several voices, one loud, came through with *"Lift me."* Near the end another loud voice said, *"Go away."* After this only one or two faint words were recorded except for the final message, when a female voice called one of the participants by name. Interestingly enough, others who have listened independently to the tape also heard this girl's name being spoken, but the girl herself did not.

In addition to the séance, I wanted to try a one-to-one experiment with a medium in touch with spirits in the next world. I worked with Robert Leichtman, M.D., a well-known psychic and author who lives in the Baltimore area. Dr. Leichtman, a specialist in internal medicine, had moved from California to work with Olga Worrall in her New Life Clinic at the Mount Washington United Methodist Church in Baltimore. The two of us had met a year earlier in connection with a case I had been investigating. I was eager for him to try to establish voice contact, via my tape recorder, with one or more of his spirit guides.

Dr. Leichtman was enthusiastic about the idea, so one evening we sat down together in my office. I first played some duplicate tapes I had made. After hearing them, he said he felt I was without question picking up genuine spirit voices.

We then tried four experiments together. Each lasted five minutes. For the first two Dr. Leichtman went into light trance, during which time he encouraged his friends to speak. At the end of each experiment, and before playback, he wrote down what he had heard while in trance. We wondered if the same messages would be on tape.

In trance Dr. Leichtman received the words, *"It's working!"* *"It works!"* *"There sure is!"* In the second experiment, after urging them to speak louder, the message, *"We're shouting,"* came back to him. The shouting message Dr. Leichtman picked up in trance is interesting. Many months after this experiment, when I was trying to explore the question of how my spirit friends get through to me, some entities said, *"We shout."*

Nothing seemed to be on tape for either experiment when we played them back.

For the third and fourth experiments we agreed that I would also ask the voices to speak. At the beginning of the second minute of the third experiment I signaled to Dr. Leichtman that I would say something. On playback, at the same moment, loud enough to be heard without headphones, a voice said, *"Next one!"*

During the last two experiments we also received *"Here."* *"I'm here."* *"Come here . . . come here,"* and *"Darien."* To me, the most interesting message was, *"Next one!"* and the implication that one or more spirits were either in the office with us and saw me motioning that I would speak or picked up telepathically that I was going to do this.

The question may arise why Dr. Leichtman, with his strong mediumistic gifts, did not receive taped voices, while I did. This is not unusual. Other mediums have sat with me for recordings. Many were confident they would get at least one taped message; yet in the majority of cases they didn't. Our contacts on the other side communicate with us in the manner in which they, and we, have become accustomed. With me it is through a tape recorder. With Dr. Leichtman it is telepathic. Other mediums have their own particular ways of getting in touch.

On a number of occasions individuals have come to my home to listen to some of my tapes, and in many instances before the evening was over, they have asked if they could try to get through to someone they once knew who died.

I approach a situation like this cautiously. You can never be sure what may be recorded, if anything. In addition, it is usually difficult to be positive that the individual called is the one speaking. The spirit world has its impostors anxious to get in on the act, so we must keep this in mind. Voices speaking to us from the next dimension have their individual characteristics, like human voices, but many times they do not sound like the voices of departed friends or loved ones as we remember them. This is easily understandable because these personalities are no longer in the body.

After explaining all of this thoroughly to my visitors, we proceed with the recording. In some cases we have been successful in getting one or more brief messages. When this has happened, most of the visitors have been sure they have heard from their loved ones.

In one situation a young woman, who had a nervous breakdown when her brother was murdered four years earlier, asked if she could try to contact him a certain evening.

During the morning recording I asked my friends on the other side to try to have Harold on hand when his sister, Jean, spoke to him that evening.

Knowing Jean's background, I was somewhat concerned about how she would respond whether Harold spoke or not. I took time first to explain carefully to her how difficult it was for those on the other side to speak, and that even if we heard nothing from Harold, it didn't mean he wasn't with us or was unaware that she was trying to get through.

Jean seemed to accept this and said she understood Harold might not be able to speak, but she was anxious to tell him she hadn't forgotten him and she still loved him.

The recording went well. Jean spoke simply but movingly to her brother, telling him how much he was missed by the family and that they all loved him and hoped he was happy.

On tape playback there were two clear messages about a minute apart. The first was, *"I love you,"* and the second was, *"Love you."*

The joy Jean showed when she heard these messages is hard to describe. She said the voice sounded like Harold's, especially in the second message, and she is convinced it was he.

Another time a woman and her daughter came to listen to a demonstration tape. At the conclusion the woman's daughter asked if she could call on her maternal grandmother, with whom she had been close. Since the mother, whom we will call Mrs. Smith, seemed agreeable to this, we proceeded with a five-minute recording. On playback there was one message: *"I'm busy."*

Mrs. Smith was thrilled. She told us that since her mother

had died five years earlier, she has had three vivid dreams about her. In each dream the mother would tell her clearly, *"I'm happy. I'm busy."* That we now had, *"I'm busy,"* on tape seemed good evidence that the grandmother had spoken.

In a different situation I met a woman, Mrs. B., at a conference who asked me to try to get through to her daughter's fiancé. He had been killed in an automobile accident a month before they were to be married. The daughter had turned to the Bible for solace at the time. This was all to the good, but when she read "whosoever believeth in him should not perish, but have everlasting life" (John 3:15), she became distraught. Since her fiancé had been from the East and a member of the Islamic religion, she was afraid he hadn't survived death.

When I returned home, I made more than one attempt to get through to him. Several messages came back that were appropriate to the situation and the questions asked. I duplicated these and mailed them to Mrs. B, stressing that while we couldn't be sure it was her daughter's fiancé, we could hope that it was, and because of the nature of the messages, there was a reasonable possibility they had come from him.

On an overcast fall day I took my battery-operated tape recorder and went to a large cemetery a few miles from where I live. I had never tried an outside recording, but I felt the results, if any, might be interesting.

As I drove around this cemetery, which I had never visited before, I looked for two things. One, I wanted to conduct my experiment in as isolated a spot as possible—not only because it would ensure quiet, but also because I was concerned what the grounds keeper might think or do if he saw an unknown woman beside a grave talking into a tape recorder. The second thing I looked for was a new grave. It was my thought that whatever faint chance I had to record a voice there would be enhanced if the person had recently died. Finally I found a site that met both requirements. The mound of the grave was still high, and there were a dozen baskets of flowers strewn over the yellow clay.

The one recording I made lasted about ten minutes. Sitting on the concrete bench beside the grave of this man I had never known, I wondered if he or anyone would, or could, speak. I waited until I had returned to my office to play the tape back, where I could run it through the cassette player with the amplifier and equalizer. I found then that I had recorded voices.

I feel that because of the differences in voices and messages, two spirits spoke. In reply to my first question about whether this was the place where the individual was buried, the answer *"Yes. I am,"* came back. My second question was whether he was happy in the spirit world. This was answered with, *"I am."*

I turned the microphone over to anyone who wanted to speak. A different voice then spoke, saying, *"Hello . . . o . . . o."* Two counters later the same voice added, *"I want to come back."*

I believe spirits do not "live" at cemeteries. They can move around freely, and when I visited the grave of this unknown individual, he and whoever else was with him showed their ability to speak. That they can continue to speak to us wherever we are, is significant.

In October, WMAR-TV, the Baltimore NBC affiliate, called and asked if they could film me at work taping voices. They would use this as a news feature at the end of the six and eleven o'clock news the evening of November first. I had appeared on a talk show for the same station in the middle of July, during which my work with the electronic voice had been presented to the public. This time they wanted to do the filming in my office. They would show me, surrounded by my equipment, talking to spirits, and, they hoped, with spirits talking to me.

I stressed how unlikely it would be for a spirit to come through at the exact moment the camera was running. Spirits do not produce on demand, and you can never be sure who may speak or when.

The special news feature editor said he understood this, but at least they could show me working. Perhaps I could duplicate some of the clearest voices for them, and they would include these on tape as examples of the voices. A date was set to film a week later.

I began urging my friends on the other side to try to speak during the program. Not leaving anything to chance, I pointed out to them how impressive this would be and that it would help get their story across. During the week, each time I asked them to speak for the program, they assured me they would help.

The morning the show was to be filmed I made two recordings before the camera crew arrived. Styhe had told me earlier, *"If you want, I will come."* I told Styhe I would call on him first. This is what I did, and in a Class A voice, picked up by my tape recorder as well as the equipment from WMAR, Styhe said, *"I will be down."*

It is fortunate that the program wasn't being filmed live, for when the crew heard Styhe, they were almost beside themselves with excitement. I told them Styhe was indicating by his message that he was in my office. With that, all of the lights in the office flickered off for two seconds. When that happened, the camera crew decided they'd had about enough and wanted to pack it up. Only the "gentle" persuasion of the special news feature editor convinced them otherwise.

During the second recording experiment we made, I invited the crew to call on someone in the spirit world to try to come through. One of them called on a friend named Gordie and said if he was standing by, now was the time to make his presence known. In a little less than a minute a fast voice said, *"I don't know what to do, velum, Gordie."*

Although the message was not as loud as Styhe's, it was clear, and by using the equalizer, we could bring it out. The crew member who had called on Gordie was stunned to have him respond, but to him, as well as to me, the use of the word *"velum"* was a mystery.

Later, in checking the dictionary, I found several definitions for velum. If you spell it with two *ll*'s, it is a type of writing surface. With one *l*, it becomes a veillike or curtainlike membranous partition, or a thin cloud, large in horizontal area, that is draped over or penetrated by cumuliform clouds.

This is interesting and perhaps gives us an insight into what spirits have to penetrate to come from their world to ours: "A veillike or curtainlike membranous partition." The voices tend to take us literally, especially when they first begin to speak, and this was Gordie's first time. The individual who called on him said it was now time to make his presence known. Could Gordie have been telling him he was unable to do so because of a veil between our two worlds?

Would it be possible to combine EVP and spirit photography? Could I capture on film one or more of the entities who speak to me in my office?

One evening Nancy and Ron Stallings and a friend, Kevin Mack, came to my office. The Stallings are the founders of the Maryland Committee for Psychical Research, and I have worked with them before. Nancy is a gifted medium, and her husband, Ron, has had success as a psychic photographer. As I had done before the TV sessions with WMAR, I started preparing the spirit world for the upcoming EVP–spirit photography experiments. Each time I mentioned it, I was assured they would come.

Our session went well and lasted about an hour. During this time I had my tape recorder recording, and I spoke frequently to those in the next dimension, inviting them to join us if they wished to give a message or have their pictures taken by Ron and Kevin.

Nancy had many strong feelings that entities were present during the hour. Although she normally does not go into trance, several times she felt herself on the verge of drifting off. At one point she told of feeling extremely cold from her waist down and urged Ron and Kevin to take pictures of the lower part of her body.

We had the film developed commercially, and on six of the pictures taken by Kevin there was a definite image. It was not, however, of the human form as we know it.

As the body goes through transitions after death, it will, at times, change shape. Eventually it becomes something best described as a ball of light, still retaining full—in fact, heightened—consciousness. I recognized, when I saw the pictures, that this seemed to be what we had captured.

The form is the size of a small orange, somewhat flattened. There are two pointed ends extending from the center, the bottom point slightly longer. The entity is in motion. It gives the impression, when the photographs are viewed in sequence, of spinning from Nancy's left knee, down to her right foot, before continuing up and away to the left, hovering over a small table that was between us. It reminds one of a child's whirligig toy. None of this was seen until the pictures were developed.

When the recording was played back, there were twenty-three messages on it, so it was clear we had a number of unseen entities in the office during the session, and at least one of them came through on film.

The day before, while I had been making a recording, a flash of something white had streaked between the tape recorder and me. I then asked, on tape, if this indicated the presence of one of my friends. In a Class A voice, which I have played for others, came the answer, *"Some sort of visual can come to you."* Thirty-six hours later we had this visual on film.

Once again, as when Styhe had spoken on television at my request, those on the other side showed an awareness of what I was attempting to do, an ability to plan, and a willingness to help bring this about.

A few days after receiving the photographs back from the developer, I spread them out on the desk beside my tape recorder. I then began the recording and invited the unseen to come into the office and look at the pictures. They took me at my word, because during the taping several different voices spoke. When I asked if they could see the pictures, I was told, *"That's your 'sistant."* I again repeated the same question, and someone said, *"Sure. I'm sure that we can."* I asked if the image was one of my friends, and a voice replied, *"That is Rabideu. That is, yes!"* Continuing, I asked who it was, and different voices speaking conversationally said, *"Nobody know him." "This is him?" "That's right!" "I doubt it."* I was not aware any of this had been recorded until tape playback. Each message was loud, clear Class A and has been duplicated and played for a number of individuals.

In the spring Ron Stallings called and asked if I could try to find out some information about a sailboat belonging to a friend of theirs that was docked in the Annapolis harbor. The boat seemed jinxed. One of the builders had gone insane during the building. A number of unpleasant situations had arisen since then, some appearing to be of paranormal origin. I agreed to try to contact those on the other side about the boat. Several clear messages were returned concerning the boat, including that there was *"storm damage to it."* I asked if there was a sister ship to this boat, and if so, where it was docked. *"Annapolis"* was the Class A answer. I checked with Ron about this, and he said there was a sister ship, but it was docked in New England. Two weeks later he called me and said the sister ship had just sailed into the harbor at Annapolis.

At the end of October WKTK-FM radio in Baltimore had asked the Stallings to speak on a broadcast of which the last thirty minutes was to be a séance originating from the Edgar

Allan Poe house in Baltimore. According to local lore, the house is haunted, and it was the hope of the talk show host that a ghost would manifest during the séance. I was asked to try to find out from the other side if the house is actually haunted, as well as something about the present whereabouts of Mr. Poe in the spirit world. During a two-day period I made several attempts to learn about Poe in the next dimension. At no time did I call on him directly: I only asked that someone come and talk to me about Poe and his present condition. Many interesting answers were returned. At one point while I was asking whether Mr. Poe had been surprised at what he'd found at death, a clear voice broke in and said, *"He understand it. On Febergan."*

The following day I asked for confirmation that the message I had received the day before had actually concerned Edgar Allan Poe. A loud, shrill voice said, *"I died!"* This segment was used by WKTK the night of the broadcast. It was played again by NBC Evening Magazine, TV-Philadelphia, when they presented a special about my work.

During the first recording the morning of October 31, when I asked if I had spirit friends with me, someone said, *"Febergan. We have our work."* The word *"Febergan"* was first heard the morning of October 25, and that it came back six days later I feel reinforces the two messages. It also suggests that *"Febergan"* may be a place in the spirit world, perhaps even the location where Poe now lives.

During the radio séance most of the six participants felt cool breezes, and a few of those who took part said they heard faint voices. The thousands of us in "radio land" who were listening to the program also heard voices murmuring. My thought was that the station had a noisy radio crew. Sitting in my office, twenty miles away, I taped the program. When I played the tape back through the large amplifier, twenty of these murmurs became discernible, and because of the content, they are without a doubt paranormal.

The next day during a recording I asked from where these messages had come. I was told, *"They work there in their place. They were in their house today."* Eight counters later a voice added, *"They died there!"*

There is some controversy about whether a location can be haunted. Skeptics decry such ideas, feeling that a belief in hauntings belongs to the ignorant or those from whom good sense, if they ever had it, has fled. We have evidence, though, that some locations are, in fact, haunted. The Edgar Allan Poe house, just mentioned, is one example. So many individuals have seen apparitions, or other psychical manifestations, in visiting haunted locations, that we cannot attribute all of these experiences to mass hysteria.

At times I receive phone calls from people who feel they live in a haunted house. They want me to visit their homes and confirm their suspicions. Occasionally some friends, who are also psychical investigators, and I will investigate such a house. Now and then we have to agree with the owners that they appear to have a true "haunt."

There are different types of hauntings. For the most part they are benevolent and make little impact upon the lives of those living in the house. They seem to exist side by side with the human occupants, living their own quiet lives and only occasionally making their presence known.

In a malevolent haunt the situation is different. Both types of hauntings can affect matter, but the second kind, the malevolent haunt, can seriously, even tragically, change lives.

Frequently in a location that is haunted you will find more than one ghost. They can be from different time periods and show great differences in personality.

I look upon a ghost, even one of the benign ones, as a sick personality. They are hanging on to a particular location for their own reasons. It is said that ghosts don't know they have died, and although this is often true, I have been in communication with ghosts, through my tape recorder, who were fully cognizant that they are dead.

Ghosts are usually unhappy, and yet for those ghosts who know they are dead, they would rather continue in the sad state they have more or less learned how to deal with than move on into the great unknown, the spirit world. Sometimes we are able to convince these types of personalities to move on, assuring them that friends and loved ones are waiting for them in the next dimension, and they will find happiness there.

At times those who call and ask that I come and investigate their haunted house want me to bring an exorcist along. I always refuse. In rare situations exorcism is successful, but there is the possibility of making a bad situation worse. In addition, my own inclination is to try to work personally with these unhappy personalities and help them move on to happier lives. We must show compassion not only for the living but for the unhappy dead as well. Attempting to cast out "lost" souls from a place they know, without offering them a better alternative, is cruel. Unless a ghost is ready to leave a location, any relief that comes from exorcism is only temporary.

A quick, violent, unexpected death seems to trigger something within some personalities causing them to stay around the place they died. It is more likely that these types of ghosts are the kind that haven't realized they've died. They know something has changed, but they are confused and unable to figure out what it is. Everything is still much like it had been before, but they wonder why most people seem unaware of their presence.

Point Lookout State Park in southern Maryland is a location where hundreds of violent deaths have taken place. On the Chesapeake Bay, it was used as a prisoner-of-war camp by the North during the Civil War, and many Confederate soldiers died there while incarcerated. In addition, a number of sailing vessels have sunk in the dangerous waters surrounding the park. There is a lighthouse located at the park's tip, and although the lighthouse is no longer operational, two apartments in it are occupied. The tenants of both apartments have reported seeing apparitions, hearing unexplained voices and footsteps, and finding various objects within the apartments moved at times. The park ranger and his assistants have also seen unusual and unexplained phenomena along the shores of the bay, by the cemetery on the grounds, and in other locations within the park.

On two occasions the Stallings and I visited the park and lighthouse to investigate the purported hauntings. Each visit confirmed that the location is haunted by many ghosts.

I wanted to discover if voices of these ghosts could be recorded through a tape recorder, and if so, whether there would be some indication of their being from the same or different time periods.

Several days before leaving for our second visit I asked my contacts on the other side to try to get through to the ghosts who lived at Point Lookout. I requested that they tell the ghosts we were making another visit to them, that we came in friendship to offer our help if they wanted it, and that I would be grateful if they would speak on tape. My contacts assured me they had done this. When I asked where the ghosts had indicated the best place to tape would be, a clear voice replied, *"They will be inside."*

We spent over six hours inside the lighthouse, and the following day, when I played the tapes back, I had nine messages. In one, which took place upstairs in the green bedroom, a loud, clear female voice asked, *"How long you going come here?— for I'm a spirit."* The message is interesting in several respects. First, it shows that the entity who spoke knew we had been there before by her question, *"How long you going come here?"* and then goes on to suggest our investigation of the lighthouse for its ghostly aspect was unnecessary because she's a *"spirit."*

Ghosts usually look upon investigations of their haunts as unwelcome intrusions. We have come without their invitation, and they wish we'd leave them alone.

The female who spoke further showed by her message that she knew she was dead, and that there is a distinction between a spirit and a ghost. She evidently hoped if she could convince us she was a spirit, we would lose interest and not come back.

While walking around upstairs I went into the bathroom and said, "We come as friends." Immediately a voice said, *"Help me."* A moment later a shrill voice said, *"Howie,"* and then finished with, *"I don't think of her."*

In the basement, which has been the scene of a number of paranormal manifestations, we spoke to any ghosts who might have been nearby, telling them that many years had passed since the Civil War, and that since their work here was finished, they should go on to the spirit world. An unusually loud, clear voice of a young boy replied, *"I was seeing the war."* From this it appears we had one of the soldiers with us.

As usual, none of these voices were heard until later when the tape was played back through the amplifier.

One afternoon last fall, an unknown woman we will call Mrs. Jones phoned and asked me to investigate her house, where strange and somewhat frightening events were taking place.

Several evenings earlier a number of objects in the house had started to fly around, some of them turning corners and traveling great distances. While Mrs. Jones had been standing in the kitchen, a cake of soap had flown from the upstairs bathroom down the stairs of the split-level home, and made a right turn into the kitchen, hitting her on the back. The electrically controlled garage door had gone up and down several times, and the car engine had also started twice, both by themselves. Her bedroom window had opened and shut, and the curtains had been yanked off their rod and left in tatters. All of Mrs. Jones's clothes that had been laid out on the bed of the guest bedroom in preparation for a trip to Denver the following week, had been thrown helter-skelter around the room. When she and her seventeen-year-old son, Dan, the only other person living in the house, had run up to her bedroom, in front of their eyes one of her shoes had risen from the floor and flown over to the dresser. At this time they'd heard a loud bang in Dan's bedroom and, running in there, found his door had hit the wall so violently that the doorknob had left a round hole in the wall.

Most of the flying objects had ended up downstairs in the foyer, some of them shattering upon impact, and others, even though made of glass, not having as much as a chip on them.

What had finally convinced Mrs. Jones and her son to leave was when Mrs. Jones had gone to bed, after things had quieted down, she'd found a kitchen knife stuck in her mattress. When she and Dan got into the car to drive to her nephew's, the garage door refused to operate properly, and they were held "prisoner" in the garage. The door would go up a few feet, yet each time Mrs. Jones prepared to back out, it would slam down, trapping them. Mrs. Jones, feeling desperate and thoroughly terrified by now, finally gunned the car backward the next time the door started to rise. No sooner had they gotten out than the door crashed back down, missing them by inches. Mrs. Jones said the "thing" followed them down the highway. The door opened unexpectedly on her son's side of the car, almost causing him to fall out. A few minutes later her eyeglass case flew out of her pocketbook, went across her face, and hit the window on her side.

When I asked Mrs. Jones what she thought was causing all this, she replied that she believed it might be her mother, who had died twelve years earlier. One of the first unusual occurrences had been her discovery of a book belonging to her mother, which had been stored on the closet shelf in the bedroom, lying in the bathroom. During the very active part of the manifestation, a bell belonging to her mother, now kept in the dining room, had rung violently. Another indication it might have been her mother, Mrs. Jones claimed, was one of the objects that had flown down to the foyer was a family picture that included her mother. The glass frame of the picture had not broken, and Mrs. Jones thought her mother had probably prevented its breakage.

As I listened to the unfolding story, I was not convinced it was the mother. Spirits do not usually wait twelve years to make their presence known if they are going to do so in such a violent manner. To me it sounded much more like a poltergeist.

The poltergeist phenomenon is a fascinating one, and a great deal has been written about it and many cases involving the phenomenon have been studied. We know that frequently someone between the age of eleven and nineteen is living in the home where this phenomenon occurs. When these people have been studied, it usually becomes evident that they are to one degree or another emotionally disturbed and all is not right in their world.

Trying to get some background on Mrs. Jones, I learned she had some problems of her own. Dan, whom she termed "a good boy," had a violent temper, and Mrs. Jones admitted they did a good deal of fighting. In addition, Dan's best friend, whom he had known all his life, had been killed two months earlier in an automobile accident. A month after this Mrs. Jones had taken Dan out of school, because he wouldn't attend regularly, and had him get a job. The boy had never gotten over his maternal grandmother's death, because she had cared for him the first five years of his life. Although she had been dead for twelve years, he still cried over her death and wanted to know why she'd had to leave him. He felt the same way about his best friend's death and visited the grave frequently.

Before ending my conversation with Mrs. Jones, I suggested they might be experiencing a poltergeist and that this usually took place where there was a teenager. I also indicated, since she had mentioned the less than happy situation existing between herself and Dan, that they could be creating some negative energies in the home, which might have caused the recent outbreak. Mrs. Jones was interested in this and seemed relieved that she might not have ghosts in her home.

Three evenings later Tom and Linda Roers of Annapolis, Maryland, publishers of *Second Sight*, a metaphysical magazine; my daughter Becky; and I visited the Jones home. We went well equipped with tape recorders. I had long wanted to investigate a poltergeist situation to see if voices of paranormal origin would speak through a recorder. This evening, I hoped, I would learn the answer. The Roers also took along several cameras to see if they might capture on film whatever was disturbing the Joneses.

Mrs. Jones and her son greeted us at the door with smiles and the news "It's all stopped!" When I asked what she attributed this to, she replied she had taken my suggestion and now she and Dan were being nicer to each other; they hadn't fought since she'd talked to me three days earlier.

After we were seated in the living room, Mrs. Jones again repeated that nothing had happened since she'd last spoken to me, although an unusual incident had occurred the day before on her way home from work. Since I know the unseen may speak at any time, making their own comments during a conversation, I asked if we had her permission to tape what she, and later Dan, had to say. This was readily agreed to by both of them.

Mrs. Jones works in a large government agency about twenty-five miles from where she lives. She always has the car radio on while traveling back and forth, and the previous afternoon, shortly after she left work, the music on the radio started playing over and over. At first she thought something was wrong with the record and the disc jockey would quickly correct the problem; however, this did not happen, and the same short fragment of music continued to play until Mrs. Jones reached home over twenty minutes later. She said soon after the music started to play, a voice sounding like a young child's began to sob and pleaded, *"Help me. Please help me."* The crying and pleas for help also continued, along with the music, until she was home.

When I questioned Mrs. Jones as to the gender of the voice, she replied, after a moment of thought, "Female." I also asked her at just what point in her drive home the music had started, and with some surprise she replied, "Oh! Why, it started not too far from where my mother lived."

We spent some time going over the events of the week as well as trying to get a better understanding of Dan and his problems. He had had nightmares since he was very young, and they still continued at an alarming frequency. They were always the same, with the same man chasing him in and around the house and then killing his mother with a butcher knife.

After talking to the Joneses, the group of us went through the house inviting the unseen to speak through our tape recorders. When the tapes were played back the following day in our own homes, we each discovered many male and female voices had been recorded. Some of the messages were *"We need help"* and *"Help Mary"* (both recorded while Mrs. Jones was describing the unusual incident with the car radio the day before), *"I just came by him," "Dark," "I should be near a stove," "Ralph's in here," "Footprints,"* and *"We can kill you if we want."* (The last two messages were recorded in the garage where they had experienced some problems.)

In a recent phone call to Mrs. Jones, I was assured by her that everything was quiet and she and Dan were continuing to be "nice" to each other.

What conclusion, if any, can be drawn from all of this? The Roers, Becky, and I agreed that it was still basically a poltergeist situation, in which, because of Dan's emotional problems, and the unpleasant relationship between him and his mother, they appeared to be bringing the entities into their home. These entities, not very far advanced in the spirit world scheme, were "feeding" on the negative energies created by Dan and his mother.

Unlike the usual poltergeist case, the incident, such as the one with the car radio, had occurred when Dan, whom we felt was the focus for the poltergeist phenomena, was far away. The car radio incident, if genuine, moved from poltergeist to spirit, in my opinion.

But was it genuine? Might Mrs. Jones have merely been telling a good story or have imagined the whole situation? During the three hours we spent in their home, Mrs. Jones and Dan gave no indication they were fabricating any part of what they were describing.

Those in unseen realms are fully capable of changing radio signals and of impressing their voices on radio programs. For those of us who use a radio for a background sound source, the altering of radio signals is almost a daily occurrence. We also must not forget the messages I taped while Mrs. Jones spoke about what had happened: *"We need help"* and *"Help Mary."* Both reinforce what she said.

In the fall WJZ-ABC TV-Baltimore, requested the Roers and I take part in a feature of the Evening Magazine program. They wanted to show Linda and me asking questions of a Ouija board in a two-hundred-year-old farmhouse in the Annapolis area. I have reservations about the Ouija, and although occasionally apparently genuine information comes through, for the most part I question purported Ouija messages from the other side. In any case, Linda and I agreed to give it a try.

During the session, which took place at night, with lights low and fire blazing in the fireplace, Linda and I asked a number of questions about any spirits who might be present. My small battery-operated tape recorder was on the floor beside me recording the fifteen-minute Ouija attempt. At one point, when Linda requested "Please tell us your name if you lived here in the 1800s," the Ouija spelled out the name "Frank." Later, on tape playback, at the exact time Linda asked her question and "Frank" appeared on the board, a tonal male voice spoke on tape the word *"Frank."*

We have seen by the séance, sessions with mediums, visitors to my office, a trip to the cemetery, Styhe's ability to come through on television, spirit photographs, the probing of a "jinxed" sailboat, a radio broadcast, the visit to a haunted state park and lighthouse, the poltergeist phenomenon, and finally, the session with the Ouija board, that these voices are responsive to us. The spirits have shown that if they want to speak, and are able, they will do so anywhere, under any conditions, with anyone who calls upon them. They are everywhere; they surround us; they are with us; they are a part of life itself. They have never left.

Chapter 8—The Voices Demonstrate Clairaudient, Clairvoyant, Precognitive Abilities

And let in knowledge by another sense.
                                        —John Dryden

Clairaudience—hearing by paranormal means

Clairvoyance—extrasensory visual perception of an object, person, or event taking place

Precognition—paranormal knowledge of something to occur in the future that cannot be explained as inference from what is already known

Nearly every day the voices on the other side show they have clairaudient abilities. They also frequently demonstrate that they are clairvoyant and, at times, are aware of something precognitively.

I feel that the fact that so many of my questions are answered demonstrates clairaudience. The voices hear what I ask and they answer more often than not. There are some experimenters who say those on the other side do not hear us. Instead they pick up our questions telepathically, and come back with answers. This does happen to a certain degree, but most certainly it is not the whole story. I know they are capable of hearing what goes on. Those on the other side seem to have devices which they refer to as "ears" to assist them in hearing us. What percentage of their responses result from hearing us clairaudiently and what percentage is from telepathic abilities is difficult to say. I suspect some spirits, like us humans, are more skilled telepathically than others, and perhaps "ears" are not as important to them. Many, however, seem to rely upon these "ears" and complain if there aren't enough to go around.

As an example, in June an unknown entity by the name of Peggy, who has spoken to me many times, came through. Although I have been unable to find out very much about Peggy, she has told me she had a husband and children and still enjoys sewing in the spirit world. She drops in now and then and speaks in a firm, clear voice. So it happened in the middle of June when she announced her presence as usual with *"Here's Peggy."*

In the second recording I told her I was happy to hear from her again and asked how she spent her time in the spirit world when she wasn't sewing.

Peggy evidently knew I was speaking to her, but she was unable to make it out, for she said, *"I can't hear."*

Two counters later a male voice said, *"We don't have enough ears."*

Three mornings after this, when I asked if they used mechanical devices called ears in order to hear us, someone replied, *"I hear you,"* and added the message previously mentioned, *"Good morning. Estep's rolling."*

In July I explored further with the spirits the question of their hearing what we say. I asked if they used something similar to our headphones in order to hear us. *"That's right!"* came back.

A friend who has spent time studying the voices is of the opinion that they never actually hear what we say. Instead they pick up each of our questions telepathically, as we ask it, and come back with the answer. The following morning during a recording I asked if this is what happens. A voice of unusual rhythm and quality said, *"That is not possible."*

Twenty-four hours later, trying to get as specific an answer as possible, I asked if they hear our questions as we talk. A clear voice replied, *"We heard you."* Later, during the same recording, I asked if it was also possible for them to telepathically pick up our thoughts. Someone said, *"Yes, we do."*

Here we seem to have two conflicting answers, which is not at all unusual in voice recordings: One said, *"That is not possible,"* and the other said, *"Yes, we do."* This suggests that sometimes our voices are heard and at other times our thoughts get through to the world beyond.

One incident that seems to prove the spirits hear what is happening occurred last spring. When you start to record, it is necessary to turn the volume control of your amplifier down completely or the microphone will send out an oscillating, shrieking sound not far removed from the sounds emergency vehicles make at their loudest. I had neglected to do this one morning, and immediately the noise filled my office. Before I could switch the volume control to OFF, a clear, fast voice asked on the tape, *"What was that?"*

If they had reached into my mind telepathically, they would have known, for I knew at once what had happened. But they didn't. They heard an unusual sound they were unable to identify, and, like us under similar circumstances, wondered what it was.

Every so often I impose upon the good nature of my friends in the next dimension by singing to them. For the most part they try to be patient and kind, but I have never heard any applause. One of my favorite songs is "Amazing Grace," and until recently I usually started with that. Before beginning, I would get out the hymnbook and announce that I was going to sing "Amazing Grace" for them and if they would like to sing along with me, I would be very happy to have them do so.

This is what happened near midnight last April: While I was singing a voice said, *"You've got to help her."*

It is true that my singing needs help, and whether they meant it in that respect, or that someone was urging another entity to join along in the songfest, we can't know. One thing seems clear: They seemed to hear me singing.

Nine days later I tried the same thing. This time, after I had sung five or six words, a voice came in with the strong, accented rhythm of the song itself and said to someone else, *"You owe it to her. Try it."* The others didn't, but here again, they must have heard me singing to them.

A few days later I sang "Amazing Grace" for the third time

and, as usual, invited them to sing along. This time, when I had finished, a voice told me, *"You're not going to get one,"* evidently meaning I was not going to find anyone willing to sing with me.

I stopped singing for two months.

In June, deciding I shouldn't allow my feelings to be so easily hurt, I again got out the hymnbook and turned to "Amazing Grace." The tape recorder was recording during this time, since I had turned the microphone over to anyone who wished to speak. I sat quietly for several minutes, book on the table beside me, before announcing that I was going to sing and extending the usual invitation for them to join in.

On playback two voices were heard. The first female voice asked, before I started to sing and during the time the microphone was turned over, *"Do you have a new song?"*

Two minutes later, as I was singing, a different female voice came in with, *"She's going good,"* and without a pause the first voice, who'd asked for a new song, said, *"She's going flat."*

I find this capsule incident exciting, for it demonstrates within several minutes some important capabilities of our spirit friends.

First, they "saw" me clairvoyantly with the hymnbook open on the table. They even seemed to see and know what hymn I had turned to, for the one entity asked for "a new song."

Then, when I began to sing, there were two different spirits, talking together conversationally, expressing differences in opinion and stating judgments they reached by hearing me singing clairaudiently: *"She's going good." "She's going flat."*

The second opinion was accurate, for I always tend to sing flat.

Some will say that they picked up from me telepathically that I was going flat. We can't dismiss this; however, at no time did I think I was "going good." Because of the way the two messages came about, I feel both were a result of clairaudience.

In the second recording I asked if they had seen me with the hymnbook open before I started to sing. A low male voice replied, *"You can say that,"* and two counters later repeated, *"You can say that."*

When I asked if they sing songs in the spirit world, and this is spelled phonetically because I don't know what it means, someone said, *"Oui, en breker en verge."*

The following morning, since they had asked for a new song, I decided to sing one for them. After I had finished, two or three voices spoke. The first one said, *"I like that."* A minute or so later a different voice said, *"Estep sang,"* and this was immediately followed with, *"Yes, she did."*

Occasionally someone on the other side will have a conversation with me, but unfortunately I am not aware of this until tape playback, or I would be more responsive to what is being said. An example of this happened in the spring. I asked one evening if I had friends with me, and someone replied, *"I don't really think so. I didn't really look."* A moment later, when I asked who was there, the speaker, evidently having looked around and seen an entity present, said, *"Here's Sam."*

In a second incident I was signing off one morning, and as I said "Thank you for speaking to me this morning" a voice said, *"That's right."* I went on to say "I hope you will come back again." The same monotone voice assured me, *"Yes, I will."* I ended by saying I hoped other friends would also be able to speak next time. With this, the voice heard in the first two messages told me, *"You have only got just me."*

There is no doubt in my or anyone else's mind who has heard the recording, that some unknown entity on the other side was having a conversation with me and was responding clairaudiently to every remark I was making. The voices not only hear me clairaudiently but they see me clairvoyantly.

A few years ago, while the tape recorder was recording in my office, I was walking around in another part of the basement, trying to decide where to put a new cedar chest. After several minutes I went into my office, turned off the tape recorder, and played the tape back. My walking around was clearly heard, and just as clear was a voice telling me to *"turn right."* While it is true that I thought briefly about putting the cedar chest in the furnace room, which would have been to my right, and which they might have picked up from me telepathically, it is also possible they saw me walking around and felt the furnace room would be a good place for the cedar chest.

In January I left the room for a few minutes after turning the microphone over to anyone who wished to speak. On tape playback, my footsteps leaving the room were heard and then someone asking loudly, *"Where's she going?"*

This must be an example of clairvoyance and not telepathy. I knew when I left the room I was going to put the wash in the dryer. Whoever spoke showed he hadn't picked up this thought but had seen me leaving.

Six weeks later there was a similar clairvoyant experience. I had again left the room, and this time before leaving I turned off the tape recorder. I did not mention I was leaving, as I usually do, but just went. When I returned, I began the second recording for the morning, and while I was giving my customary introduction, which is the date, time, and my name, someone broke in, sounding like my unknown friend of six weeks earlier, and asked, *"Where'd you go?"* It is obvious he knew I was gone, but he didn't know, as I did, where I had been. What I find most puzzling about the incident is why he didn't "track" me clairvoyantly up to the kitchen and see me putting the breakfast dishes away. Most spirits who speak show an ability to go with me and see clairvoyantly what I am doing.

One evening last summer desire overcame willpower, so I walked up to the boardwalk in the seashore town where I stay, and bought a box of caramel popcorn. I always feel guilty when I do that sort of thing, and going on the philosophy that the faster I eat it, the shorter time my guilt will last, I stuff it down quickly. Before beginning to record I had a marvelous time reading and eating a large part of the popcorn. An hour or so later I began the first recording, and in fewer than thirty seconds someone sang to me in a loud, clear voice, *"You love popcorn!"*

What can you say after something like that? I feel occasionally like the proverbial fish in a fishbowl. For some time I have known there is little I do of which my friends on the other side are unaware. This for the most part gives me a warm, comforting feeling, but at the same time I wish, now and then, they would be a little more tactful.

It is nice to receive compliments, whether from human or spirit friends. Sometimes the compliments from those in the next dimension show clairvoyance. On the night of July ninth, I had signed off for the evening and someone told me, *"Look good tonight."*

The following morning I asked if they had said the evening before that I looked good. Immediately a male voice repeated the message given twelve hours earlier, *"Look good tonight,"* and one counter later added, *"That's so."*

One evening at the end of October I wore a new housecoat while recording. After finishing the recording session, I allowed the tape to run for a few seconds for any last message someone might want to give. During this time an entity said clearly, *"You look real pretty."*

Two months ago I tried several experiments using a wireless microphone. The experiments did not turn out as hoped and I soon discarded the idea. Two days later I made a recording using a regular mike. As I was discussing the experiment I had done two evenings earlier and how unsatisfactory it had been on tape, a voice sounding like Styhe's broke in and said, *"Saw it. Was in office with you."*

Another incident, which shows a clairaudient and possibly clairvoyant awareness, involved my Aunt Jane. Shortly after her death she said she would be with me *"every day,"* and although I don't know if this is literally true, our close association continues.

A phone call from Jane's sister-in-law had come one evening concerning Jane's will, which was due to be probated shortly. I realized I had not seen the will for some time and thought it had been lost. After a brief but frantic search I located it and put it in a convenient place where I could find it quickly when needed.

Several days later I asked one morning if I had spirit friends with me. A clear Class A voice answered, *"Auntie Esther."* The use of the name Esther is interesting. Although my aunt's name was Esther Jane, all her friends called her Jane. I, however, always referred to her as Auntie Esther. This has continued on the other side. When her associates speak to me about her, they usually say *"Jane."* When she comes through personally, it may be as Jane or Esther. In any case, on this particular morning, I was told that *"Auntie Esther"* was with me. During this same recording, not knowing that my aunt was present, I turned the microphone over to anyone who wished to speak. A loud, clear Class A female voice said, *"I want to speak to her. The legacy."*

After playing the first recording back through the amplifier and hearing what had been recorded, I began the second recording by telling my aunt what I had just received on tape. I asked her what she wanted to say about the legacy.

The male voice heard in the first recording said, *"She's*

here." One counter later my aunt said in a Class A voice, *"Find it!"*

These messages are interesting for several reasons. First, because of the nature of the messages, I feel we have good proof that my aunt was with me. Second, she exhibited an awareness that for a brief time I had thought the will to be lost and had frantically searched for it. At the same time she also showed she didn't know I had found it.

This can perhaps be explained by the emotional turmoil I went through as I began my search, not knowing whether I would be able to locate the will. My distress must have communicated itself to my aunt in her dimension. Even though I was relieved when it was found, this feeling was not as intense as the first feeling of anxiousness. In fact, I felt somewhat disgusted with myself at having mislaid it in the first place.

The episode is further evidence that our loved ones remain aware of us and of the experiences we are undergoing. It could be that the greater the joy, or distress, associated with the experience, the more easily this can be transmitted to the world beyond.

The spirits have shown clairaudient, clairvoyant, precognitive abilities about other members of my family. Last winter my son, Bob, was upstairs playing with our dog, Misty, while I was taping. Instead of calling her Misty, he called her "honey." An unusually loud female voice sounding nearby whispered, *"Who me?"*

I have duplicated this message and played it for others. Everyone agrees on what is said, but there is a difference of opinion as to how it should be taken. It seemed clear that this female clairaudiently heard my son.

The voice sounds surprised, as if she thinks she is being called "Honey." There is also the possibility that she was teasing us. Although it has seldom happened, I have upon occasion wondered if I was being teased by the voices. Spirit wit, when it manifests, is usually of the dry sort and leaves the experimenter unsure if the unseen entity is joking or not.

The voices for the most part do not display a sense of humor. They may be lighthearted and gay, but jokes are almost unknown. Repeatedly they say they come to my office to *"work."* One morning a voice, speaking to someone else, said on the reverse side of the tape, *"If you go down to work, sit any-*

where.'' This recorded voice is of such excellent quality, I frequently end tape demonstrations with it. To them "crossing the bridge" from their world to ours is an important matter, and they approach recordings with great seriousness. Those of us who believe we talk to the spirit world through our tape recorders, and those who accept the possibility that we may, look upon this communication between two worlds as a momentous achievement. It is entirely possible that those in the world beyond feel the same way.

In July there was an incident indicating a clairvoyant awareness of my daughter Cindy. I was making my second recording on the morning of July fourth, when a distinct, close female voice said, *"Estep. Hi, Cindy! Good girl!"* All of this was Class A, and I have duplicated it onto a demonstration tape which I play for others. The story behind the message is interesting.

Cindy was spending a few days with us on vacation from her job as a legal secretary in Washington, D.C. At the time the message came through, she was upstairs packing for her return to her apartment in Arlington, Virginia.

This female entity, who knows me well, and realizes I am reluctant to accept something unless I have proof, was aware if she didn't say the word *"Estep,"* I would always wonder whether it was my daughter Cindy she was referring to, or some other Cindy. To erase any doubts I might have, she first said *"Estep."* At no time had I mentioned on tape that Cindy was home.

The spirit, realizing Cindy would be gone within an hour and wanting to tell her she was a *"good girl!"* knew she had to speak right then or lose the opportunity. This was apparently strong motivation, and she was able to bring the message through at the appropriate moment and clearly enough so there wouldn't be any doubt about it.

A week or so before, Cindy had decided to return to the University of Maryland at the beginning of the fall term to finish her degree. This is something the spirit who spoke to her would have heartily approved—thus the message *"Good girl!"*

When I heard this, I suspected the identity of the speaker. In the next recording, without revealing that I thought I knew who had spoken, I asked who had greeted Cindy in this manner. The clear Class A answer was *"Mom Wilson."* Mom Wilson was my mother.

Just a week ago there was another incident involving Cindy—a precognitive one. During a heavy rainstorm she had a serious automobile accident when the car behind her lost its brakes and plowed into the rear end of her car. Although Cindy was not injured, she was thrown across the front seat, and almost a thousand dollars worth of damage was done.

The following morning at the breakfast table Cindy asked me if inanimate objects give off auras. I replied that some people claim they do. She then told me that shortly before the accident she had had a compelling feeling not to continue on the highway but to turn left. At the same time she had seen a purple light across the steering wheel. She had ignored the impression and light and continued on her way. The light had seemed to fade away for a moment or two and then had come back brightly. A minute later Cindy's accident had occurred.

Because of my activities as a psychical investigator, Cindy is well aware of the world of psi. She, however, has never before had what could be classified as a paranormal experience, beyond the everyday type of telepathy and so on.

I told Cindy I felt her precognitive impression to turn off the highway was given to her by someone on the other side. The purple light she saw was not an aura from the steering wheel but the unseen presence of a spirit entity who first tried to get Cindy to leave the highway telepathically, and when that failed, stayed in the car to protect her from physical harm when the accident happened. It should be mentioned that Cindy was driving my mother's car, which we had inherited at her death.

Later that morning, during the first recording, I asked what the purple light was that Cindy had seen. A Class A voice replied, *"Mom Wilson was there."* The spirits added later that they had been there to keep Cindy from being hurt.

The following day, when I asked how they knew ahead of time there was going to be an accident, a loud, clear voice said, *"I can look."*

This is additional confirmation for an answer given months earlier in response to my question about how they know something precognitively. *"I look down"* had been returned at that time.

Some individuals who begin to record voices try to use them as their private pipeline to the future. They think they will be able to find out what is going to happen before it does, and nothing will catch them unawares.

The idea of precognition raises the fundamental question as to what extent our lives are planned versus how much free will we have. I think our lives hold a little of both, but I would not attempt to try to guess at the percentages of either.

Precognition does exist. It has been reported thousands of times in spontaneous experiences, and while many of these are undocumented, a number of them are and cannot be dismissed. Experiments with electronic random generators have also been undertaken under controlled laboratory conditions, which some parapsychologists feel demonstrate the reality of precognition.

In my own work with the voices I have rarely asked about the future. To start with, you never know whether the answer you receive is reliable; it all depends on who gives it.

Second, it doesn't seem right to try to use the spirits to cue you in to the future. They are more important than that. The spirits are well aware that the reason I communicate with them is to find out what the spirit world and life there are like, for my personal knowledge as well as to share it with others. They approve of this, and I am sure this is why they frequently tell me, *"We will help you."* I doubt they would cooperate the way they have if I tried to use them as my private pocket wizards.

In talking about precognition, we must keep in mind self-fulfilling prophecy. If I dream, or am told by a psychic I will wreck my car, and then do so, is it a true example of precognition or have I "self-fulfilled" that prediction? Ridiculous? So it would seem. Obviously I would not consciously wreck my car, but the subconscious is capable of astonishing and not always marvelous things.

Genuine precognition must be preknowledge of something to happen in the future unexplainable by inference from what is already known. It must be rigidly controlled so no possibility of self-fulfilling prophecy, conscious or unconscious, comes into question. The best example I can think of is of information about someone or something that will happen without your having any part in its occurrence.

Such an experience was mine several winters ago. The spirit, who may have living relatives, we will call Jack Shipley. The other gentleman involved was the well-known lecturer and author of close to seventy books, many in the field of psi phenomena, Martin Ebon.

It was January, and morning found me, as usual, at my tape recorder. I was trying to explore the question of music with my spirit friends, and my question was, "Please tell me who some of the composers are in the spirit world." In less than a minute the name "*Jack Shipley*" was recorded.

When I heard this name on playback, I wondered who he was. It was not the name of any composer I knew, however it had been spoken clearly, so I entered it into my log and decided it was a "drop-in" guest. In the next recording I turned the microphone over to Jack in case he wanted to bring a message, but nothing further was heard.

An organization I belong to was having its annual banquet that evening, and Martin Ebon was going to talk about evidence for life after death. I had tickets and looked forward to going.

During the afternoon severe weather conditions developed—first snow, then sleet, then finally, freezing rain. All the meteorologists and newscasters urged us to stay off the roads and not to travel unless absolutely necessary. Only the foolhardy would venture out. I would not be one of those, I decided, and gave up all thought of going.

The later it got, the more uneasy I became. I paced from one room to another feeling a great disquietude within myself. This is not my typical behavior, and I was at a loss to understand what was happening. I felt a compulsion to do something, but I didn't know what it was. Suddenly I stopped my pacing and said "I'm going to the banquet."

Immediately I experienced relief, as if in spite of the sleet and freezing rain outside, I had made a right decision. Rushing around, I got ready and was on my way. My destination was over an hour away, and I barely made it on time.

The group had a pleasant dinner, and then Martin Ebon rose to speak. He was informal and amusing, and his topic held interest for all of us.

Ebon spoke of different mediums he had known, the famous and not so famous, and how some seemed to be in touch with spirits and the spirit world. He admitted it was difficult at times to be sure whether they were genuine, and even for those who appeared to be, certain ones were not above fraud now and then.

Ebon continued: "One medium with whom I had close contact some years ago, and who was controversial, but I felt had genuine gifts, was Jack Shipley.''

The impact of what he said did not register for a moment, but then it did. Here was the proof, the evidence for life after death, of which he spoke. Ebon is a cautious person, as he should be. He refuses to say we have proof. What he does say is that there is increasing evidence that humans survive death.

Well and good. I join him in his cautiousness. I have questioned everything that has happened the last twelve years. I look for answers, for other explanations; I play the devil's advocate constantly; but I have become convinced that spirits do communicate and are trying to tell us they have survived.

Jack Shipley, a ''controversial medium,'' has done this from the other side. What gifts he had on the earth plane have magnified to awesome proportions. To start with, he knew precognitively that his friend Ebon was going to speak on a certain night about evidence for life after death. This is not too startling, for those in the spirit world keep in better touch with us than we do with them. The astounding part is that he somehow knew that I, whom he had never met, would be going to the banquet, would hear Ebon mention his name, and would remember that I had recorded it at eight thirty-five that morning.

We must not forget how, because of the weather, I almost didn't go—how it was only after several hours of a most unusual restlessness and inner discomfort that I changed my mind. Jack Shipley knew this and prevailed upon me in some unknown fashion to venture out into the storm. I allowed myself to be guided and received a gift of inestimable value.

Yes, the voices exhibit clairaudient, clairvoyant, and precognitive abilities. They hear us, see us, and at times know what the future will bring. If we wish, they will share their gifts with us.

Chapter 9—The Voices and Reincarnation

The soul is immortal and is clothed successively in many bodies. —Plato

Does humankind reincarnate? This question has been asked since earliest history.

We can see from the introductory quotation in Plato's *Diogenes Laertius* that he believed the soul returned to live "in many bodies." Approximately twenty-three hundred years later Friedrich Nietzsche wrote in *Thus Spake Zarathustra*: "All things return eternally and ourselves with them. We have already existed times without number, and all things with us."

Mark Twain spent much of his lifetime searching for a woman with blond hair to whom he believed he was married in another life. General George S. Patton believed he had been a Roman soldier two thousand years ago. Writer Henry David Thoreau and inventor Thomas Edison both believed they had lived other lives.

Reincarnationists are not on the lunatic fringe of humanity. Reincarnation is accepted as a matter of course by Hinduism, one of the oldest surviving major religions in the world. Many of the Tlingit Indians of southeastern Alaska also believe in it and adapt their social and religious lives to a philosophy based upon it.

Spirits do not know everything about everything; however, reincarnation is one of those areas about which I think they should know.

90

You may ask why they should be privy to the secrets of reincarnation when we are not. To start with, many young children claim to recall past lives and give evidential information about those lives. While in most cases these memories fade with age, some individuals retain them all their lives. In addition we arrive on the earth plane as infants and during the birth process seem to go through a "sea of forgetfulness." If we have lived before, memories of those lives are wiped out, in most cases, along with more recent experiences as spirits in the spirit world.

Most of us have met and talked to someone who has told us about a life he or she recalls having lived a hundred or two hundred years ago. Isn't it strange, though, that we never meet anyone who talks about a life he or she remembers living as a spirit thirty or forty years previously? Your skeptics will say this disproves the existence of a spirit world and demonstrates that reincarnation is the product of sick minds.

All we can do to decide this issue is rely on the evidence that has accumulated suggestive of reincarnation, and after careful consideration, try to draw as objective and intelligent a conclusion as possible.

Arriving in the spirit world cannot be compared to our birth on the earth plane. Most of us reach the world beyond as adults, after a lifetime of learning, with our faculties reasonably intact. We pick up where we left off on the earth plane a short while before. As we shall see in a moment, spirits seem to be given some choice in the matter of reincarnation, and this choice implies knowledge.

In spite of my expectation that spirits should know all about reincarnation, some apparently do not. William Welch in his book *Talks with the Dead* asked his spirit guide Mark if reincarnation was a reality. Mark didn't seem to know the answer but promised to return later that evening with the information. He did, and his reply was that it was not the "normal" way of things.

All I can do is present what I have received through spirit communication concerning reincarnation and let each individual make his or her own decision whether to accept, reject, or hold the verdict on the concept in abeyance.

Shortly after I started to tape voices twelve years ago, I began asking if man reincarnates. Usually I received an answer, and when I did, it was always positive. Some of these early answers were: *"Man comes back." "He can." "He comes back."*

I was satisfied with these answers, and because there were many other things I wanted to know, I went on to different subjects. From time to time I would return to reincarnation, and as the voices grew stronger and more able to express themselves, additional information was returned.

In Chapter 6 I mentioned what I felt was strong suggestive evidence of humans reincarnating via voice messages, saying that people *"go home"* to the spirit world when they die. Consequently I don't want to belabor the point again here. We should keep in mind that while no spirit talked about reincarnating back to the earth plane, this could be inferred when they say they have returned to the spirit world. In order to return somewhere, you must first have left. We also remember James's message when he said he could *"prove"* we had a *"second home."*

At the end of March I asked if everyone returns from the spirit world to the earth plane to live another life. The answer *"Yes"* was recorded in an echo effect.

In the second recording that morning I asked why if reincarnation was a fact, it was necessary for a human to come back. A female voice replied, *"He should come back."*

Two days later I asked if one commits suicide, must he return to the earth plane to live through the same situation for which he took his life? *"Yes, Estep, yes"* was recorded in a loud Class A voice.

Wanting to double-check their answer, I again asked the same question in the following recording. This time a voice answered, still Class A, *"Yes. He must want to return."*

There is a theory held by many believers in reincarnation that before a soul reincarnates back into a new earth body, it chooses the parents to whom it wishes to be born. Some of Dr. Ian Stevenson's case histories suggest this, as expressed in his book *Twenty Cases Suggestive of Reincarnation*. The idea is that we somehow look over, from the spirit world, the available homes into which we could be born. We then decide, either because of a closeness we felt with an individual in a previous incarnation or because we feel a particular home environment is what we need to further our personal development, to be reborn to that person or into that home. I have always found this difficult to accept. In March, when I asked whether one chose one's parents before birth, in spite of my thoughts on the matter, someone replied, *"Yes."*

Another theory is that while in the spirit world, we can choose what direction we want our life to go when we are reborn on the earth plane. In other words, if we wish to come back with the capability of becoming a musician, we can. I asked about this and was told, *"That's not quite right."*

The transmigration of the human soul as it returns from the spirit world to the earth plane is of concern to many. Does it come back to inhabit a human body, or does it at times, as some religions believe, go into an animal body?

In April I asked if the soul was always reborn as a human personality. In strong rhythm someone said, *"That's right. Thank you."* Since the spirits evidently wanted to be sure I had recorded this particular message correctly, thirty seconds later they supplied an additional message: *"Get right!"*

In May a somewhat amusing and puzzling incident transpired. I had asked who was with me one morning, and three messages came: The first was, *"Up. I come to speak,"* a minute later, *"This is Ben,"* followed immediately with, *"This is Franklin."* The last two messages were Class A, and there was no ambiguity with their interpretation.

What or whom did I have here? Benjamin Franklin? Not standing on ceremony, I asked in the second recording if I had possibly heard from Benjamin Franklin.

A most unusual voice, with rare emotional quality, shrieked, *"He's still on earth!"*

Not knowing that this message had been recorded, I went on to ask Mr. Franklin if he had a message for me. *"I feel fine,"* someone said. These messages were good Class A and easily understood.

So whom do we have? Benjamin Franklin himself, or an impostor? While we can't categorically rule out Mr. Franklin, I am inclined to feel it was an impostor. It is interesting that our "tricky" spirit chose Franklin. Why not someone of more recent times? One of my ancestors, James Wilson, was a friend and associate of Mr. Franklin. It could be that the spirit entity tuned in to my subconscious somehow and, picking this up, decided to give me a thrill.

It is worthy of notice that someone on the other side heard this exchange between the so-called Mr. Franklin and me. He was evidently so upset at the idea that I might accept the communication at face value that his voice, shrieking in a tonal quality I had never heard before, or since, told me that Franklin had returned to the earth.

Benjamin Franklin believed in reincarnation. At the early age of twenty-two he had written his own epitaph in which he showed not only that he accepted the idea of reincarnation but that he was anxious to return. He wrote "The Work shall not be lost, for it will, (as he believ'd) appear once more, In a new and more elegant Edition, Revised and corrected, by the Author."

The message *"He's still on earth,"* besides showing that the spirits are aware of whomever and wherever we are, is, I feel, additional "unconscious" evidence for the reality of reincarnation. Like the *"go home"* messages from those who speak to us from the world beyond, the notion of reincarnation cannot be denied, and the "unconscious" mention of it by the spirit voices make its reality all the stronger.

I have had extended contact with an individual by the name of Jeffrey from the next dimension who says he was my brother in a previous life. At first I dismissed such claims as those of someone using a novel way to get my attention. I can no longer do this so easily. Over the years he has spoken to me, I have come to feel very close to him. When my world is not going well, Jeffrey will almost invariably announce his presence by clearly saying his name. He tells me repeatedly he is in my office, and unlike with most of the others who speak, I can sense his presence when he is nearby. The other spirits seem to know Jeffrey. More than once shortly before he says his name I have recorded, *"Here's her brother,"* or *"Here's Jeffrey."* Recently I asked if Jeffrey and I would meet face-to-face when it came time for me to return to the spirit world. An excellent Class A voice indicated this would probably happen by saying, *"We have marked him."* During the spirit photography session, when I asked who was there, someone said, *"Jeff. We saw him. That is good."*

Last spring I asked if it was possible for a person who has out-of-body experiences to visit other realities. The answer came back in an accented monotone: *"Yes. This is freeze-back, but you don't know it."* At the time, although I found the answer interesting, I dismissed it as beyond my comprehension.

More recently, when I called upon Jeffrey, someone indicated he had gone into freeze-back. I asked Styhe what the term meant, and he replied in a loud voice with rhythm: *"Went before him."* The following morning he added, *"I see with it."*

Trying to tie everything together, I then asked Styhe if he meant that one who goes into freeze-back could see or relive what went before one in a previous life. *"Yes"* was said several times.

A few gifted persons on this plane have the ability of retrocognition. This is an extrasensory perception of past events unexplainable by present knowledge. From what I understood Styhe to relate about freeze-back, perhaps some individuals in the next dimension have the ability to look into the past, and in the looking, see part of their former lives.

Could there be any relation between out-of-body experiences used to visit other realities and freeze-back used to visit past lives? Immediately I was struck by the thought that in both situations one enters a reality discrete from the here-and-now consciousness of whatever dimension one belongs.

As a whole, my attempts to learn from Jeffrey and others something about their past lives on the earth plane have met with disappointment. Most seem vague about what happened in earlier existences. If we have lived numerous lives, as some claim, then it may not be surprising to forget the details of previous incarnations. The "sea of forgetfulness" may work on both sides of the "veil."

With such a profound philosophical question as reincarnation I hesitate to assume the position of omniscience. All I feel I can say is that the evidence I have accumulated permits me personally to accept it. I doubt anyone will ever be able to prove conclusively that reincarnation is or is not a reality. We must each, in the end, travel our own road and try to find our own answers to that which is of concern to us, whatever they may be.

Chapter 10—What We Can Learn from the Voices

Those who speak from the next world show a wide range of interests. The difficulty in crossing from one dimension to the next is always with us, and yet, in spite of this, the spirits have managed to communicate enough information to us that the spirit world is emerging from the shadow in which it has so long been shrouded.

Spirits have a far greater ability than we do to transcend the barriers separating our two worlds. In has been my fortune to be on the receiving end of many of their transmissions.

From the beginning I have explained to them why I wanted to be in contact with their world. They, taking me at my word, have made me very much a part of it.

They do not try to disguise the world beyond and show it as a perpetual place of love and laughter. It would not have been difficult for them to keep the darker side hidden. All of those who cry for help, who show that hate and thoughts of violence at times occur, could have been kept off the channel. That was not what they, or I, wished.

No, I wanted to know as much as possible about the next dimension, the bad along with the good. The countless questions I have asked have brought many answers, all of which have helped me gain an insight into this world, only a step away from ours. There has also been a tremendous amount learned from "sitting in" on various situations taking place at a given moment in the spirit world. It was as though whoever was controlling the recording on the other side decided to permit my presence. In any case, they didn't pull the switch, for which I am grateful.

I am constantly amazed at how much those on the other side are like us; they are still human personalities despite their expanded capabilities. Like us, some use these capabilities more than others.

The following voice messages are examples of spirit replies to my opening request at each recording session: "Please tell me if I have friends present."

"Yes, Estep."

"Yes, you have. Ken, Ken, Calif."

"Serving Band. Helping."

"You almost through."

"I'm dead."　　*"Help you."*

"I know good thing."

"Herr Hufbaron."

"I don't know him."

"This is very different. You should come."　　*"That's right."*

"Just me."

"Here is Gladys."

"Hello. I hope so."　　*"This is Jean Pruitt."*　　*"Thank you."*

"You are tested."

"Hope to thank you."

"Yes. I'd like to speak to you."

"Yes, she's a new one."

"You have some other vacuum with you."

"Estep, you have."

"Here's Fräulein."　　*"I'm Fräulein."*

"Yes, right here."

"We talk to you."

"Estep, merci."

"Four. We're here again."

"Get him to speak. Get him speak."　　*"Wait!"*

"You have friends."

"Did he say he's coming?"

"Have six."

"Mrs. Johnson talked too long."   *"I heard you."*

"Three. I find three."

"You have me."

"Hello, Sally."

"I'm second."   *"Yes. I am first."*

"Have seven."

"Yes. Can you hear me?"   *"You come back
    here."*   *"And reveal yourself coming."*

"You take care of Edgar Cayce."

"I can say that we love to channel it."   *"We can say
    that we actually do."*

"That is true."

"You have the Myers."

"Yeah."   *"Yes, come down through
    space."*   *"You're right."*

"Hold my hand."

"Yes, four guys."   *"We don't really got."*   *"Walk
    down from there."*

"Eileen."   *"Dean here."*

"The Baron Saysegey."

"Near the clock."

"You still like me."

Most of these individuals had nothing further to say when given the opportunity later, with some exceptions. These back-and-forth exchanges of questions and answers are good demonstrations of the two-way conversations that take place at times.

When I asked what the Serving Band was, someone replied, *"Helping God."*

I wanted to know if the "good thing" they mentioned affected me, and if so, what it was. *"It's going to"* was the answer.

I told Herr Hufbaron if there was anyone he would like me to greet in his name, I would be happy to do so. In a loud voice he said, *"Right! Otto Pushkin."*

I had to wonder if he was any relation to Aleksandr, but in any case his whereabouts remain unknown.

When I later called on Gladys, she responded, *"Hello . . . hello . . . hello. I missed you."* During the same recording I asked who she was. A different voice answered, *"That's good question."*

Twenty-four hours after the *"You are tested"* message, I asked them for what they were testing me. *"Your ability,"* a male voice replied.

The statement, *"You have some other vacuum with you,"* is a fascinating one. You will remember that they have used the word *"vacuum"* at other times. It always sounded the same, slow and drawn out— *"vac-u-um."* At first the message suggested to me that those who spoke did so by entering a vacuum. I explored this question with them thoroughly over the weeks and months that followed. For a long time I got positive responses, many of them Class A. In the recording after the *"You have some other vacuum with you"* message, I asked if they meant my friends placed themselves in a vacuum in order to speak. *"That's it"* was the answer. During this same recording I asked how they created a vacuum, and the long, puzzling answer, most of it Class A, came back: *"Requires truck and to exiting into limb through a vacuum you enter from truck."*

In the third recording that morning I asked if they created a vacuum in their world much as we do here. *"Yes. That's right!"* was taped. I also asked if it was necessary for them to create a vacuum in order to speak to us. Someone sang in a clear voice, *"Yes, we do that."*

Four months later I asked Styhe if he had been having difficulty lately creating a vacuum, and he answered, *"Infrequent."* In the next recording I asked him if he had meant they create vacuums infrequently. Styhe's female associate said, *"Do not do that,"* and ten counters later Styhe came in with, *"We don't like to do that. We don't have."*

Do they create vacuums in order to speak to us or don't they? I have talked to my more scientifically inclined friends about vacuums, and they tell me in a perfect vacuum sound waves cannot be transmitted.

Why the *"You have some other vacuum with you"* message then? Perhaps they meant vacuum in a different context than the way I took it. Although the voices reinforced the vacuum concept in subsequent recordings and seemed definite about it, it remains an enigma.

When I turned the microphone over to Fräulein in the recording I made after she spoke, a female voice said, *"I am here. Yes, I am. I am here."*

Twenty-four hours after the message, *"Four. We're here

again," I asked if they could tell me who the four were. *"We can"* was the loud reply. They didn't but perhaps they had taken my question literally. If I had phrased it differently, such as "Please tell me who you are," I might have received some names.

That is what I did with the *"Have seven"* message. I asked them to tell me the names of the seven who were in my office. *"Poppy York,"* a name I have recorded before, was the answer.

The *"You take care of Edgar Cayce"* message is interesting. I accept it as genuine because the voice did not claim to be Edgar Cayce. It was speaking to someone else, as if to say they should help Mr. Cayce come and observe the recording. Unfortunately I didn't realize until a week later that I had recorded the message about Cayce. I apologized on tape for this and said if I had known Mr. Cayce was with me, I would have called on him to speak. I then went on to ask where he was in the spirit world. A loud Class A voice came back with *"Clarify that."* A few counters later a different voice, still Class A, returned, *"That's my man. Disciple."*

As one of the most impressive mediums who ever lived, Mr. Cayce continues to have an interest in proving postmortem survival. Robert Leichtman, M.D., wrote a series of books titled *Heaven to Earth*. Well-known personalities who have died communicated through the mediumship of D. Kendrick Johnson, a close friend of Dr. Leichtman. In the first book of the series, *Edgar Cayce Returns*, Dr. Leichtman wrote interestingly about the long conversations he had with Cayce when Cayce spoke through the entranced Mr. Johnson.

The long message about "channeling it," evidently meaning communications between the spirit world and this world, was spoken by three voices, two male and one female. Each part of the message was given in uneven tempo, and for the last two parts there were double knocks before the entities spoke. It was more as if they were having a conversation among themselves than speaking to me.

In the next recording I asked if they had the capability to tune in to whomever they wished to on the earth plane. Still Class A, someone's voice replied, *"Yes, we do."*

When I asked the Myers if they had a message for me, they answered, *"Thank you. I hope that we can help you."*

For the most part I try to guide each recording session along the area I want to explore. Every day or two, though, I turn the microphone over to those on the other side who have their own messages to bring. The following messages, all Class A, have come in response to my saying "The microphone is yours."

> *"It's different."*
> *"Help me."*
> *"Sally, Sally, hello."*   *"Recording."*
> *"Not time yet."*
> *"Come through."*   *"Let Doll through."*   *"What can I say to?"*
> *"Estep."*
> *"My telephet."*   *"Get through."*
> *"Sally, I love you."*   *"Good night."*
> *"Very sad."*
> *"Happy."*   *"Okay if we talk to you."*
> *"I want to talk to you. I'm a doctor."*
> *"Margo."*   *"You will wake the nether!"*
> *"I'm listening. I'm listening."*   *"Get in this house. Get in this house."*
> *"Don't you ask who's always talking?"*
> *"Guess what!"*   *"Yes."*   *"You're now spidelade on it."*
> *"There's somebody loose back there."*
> *"Let someone speak."*
> *"Corey tried to."*
> *"This sad home."*
> *"We thank you."*
> *"Help me move out."*

I respond to each message given, and sometimes there is additional communication from the other side. The background of some of the messages is also interesting.

On June twentieth one of my daughters underwent major surgery; at 8:55 that evening the *"I want to talk to you. I'm a doctor"* message came through. The male voice was loud and clear and had unusual vocal quality. He evidently knew about my daughter and was letting me know he was standing by.

Once a Spiritualist minister came to my home to listen to voice tapes. During the evening she said she saw an entity by the name of Margo. I knew no one by that name, but within a day or two I called on Margo, and she responded. She has a clear voice and usually replies when called upon, but for the most part offers only her name. At 9:45 A.M. on June twenty-sixth, when I had turned over the microphone, she replied in her usual loud, strident voice *"Margo."* Three counters later a different voice chided her: *"You will wake the nether!"* This affords us a brief glimpse of spirit psychology. Although there are exceptions, most spirits do not look upon themselves as dead.

"I'm listening. I'm listening."   *"Get in this house. Get in this house"* was a conversation between a female and a male voice. It is interesting how both of them repeated their message.

"Don't you ask who's always talking?" is also thought-provoking, for the conversers seem to be reminding me I neglected to do this one morning. After asking whether I have friends with me, I then go on to request that they tell me who is there. In the next recording that morning I asked who had given the message, and someone said in an emphatic voice, *"You'll be asking just one."*

An entity by the name of Corey Bingham has spoken to me many times. He followed me from Maryland to New Jersey and back to Maryland again at the end of the summer. He has a clear voice, and I have tried to establish firm communication with him, but for some reason, we still remain out of step with each other. All he has been able to tell me about his past is that he met me at a picnic—an event of which I have no recollection.

On this particular evening I had said I would like to hear from anyone who had a message for me. In a slightly reproving voice someone told me, *"Corey tried to."* I then asked whether the message had come from the spirit world: *"Yes"* was taped.

The next morning I asked the voices to please try to get Corey for me. Many voices were heard in the background, and then someone said, *"Corey Bingham."* One counter later *"Thank you. Wait now"* was taped. I then went on to ask if he was with me, and *"Come in"* was heard.

The end of each recording is another time many voices decide to speak. It is as if they realize it is now or never and plunge in with whatever is on their minds during the few seconds I permit the tape to run before turning off the recorder.

The following Class A messages have come after I announced "This recording is ending."

> *"Thank you."*
> *"I want to."*
> *"Hope to see you."*
> *"You're very pretty."*
> *"I'm looking pretty."*
> *"You make us unhappy once you leave."*
> *"Good night, Estep."*
> *"Yes, recorded."*
> *"That's not right."*
> *"We try to give help!"*
> *"This drum it seems to fail."*
> *"La bravé great salesman. Bigs bra bravit."*
> *"Have a good night."*
> *"We really like you. You're very pretty. We count you."*
> *"That's much better. Yes, it will help me."*
> *"Gut night."*
> *"We treasure her."*
> *"Estep."*
> *"Let me thank you."*
> *"I was going say. Come again."*
> *"Hello. If you want, I will come."*
> *"What do you think? I are regret."*
> *"Where you going?"*
> *"With you. That's not clear."*
> *"Take a walk after ten. Margo."*
> *"She's pulled out from me."*   *"What you say?"*
> *"We'll be seeing you."*   *"We can't promise to do that."*
> *"Have we got one of the faithful?"*
> *"Wait for me."*
> *"Take a portrait."*
> *"I'll be here."*
> *"Come back."*
> *"Good night!"*

In the next recording, which usually runs from twelve to twenty-four hours later, I sometimes respond to what was said earlier. In most cases, because of the time lapse, there is no answer, but there have been a few surprising exceptions. These exceptions, I feel, help prove that at least some entities on the other side remain aware of us all the time and know when we have returned to the tape recorder.

The background of some of the examples I have given is interesting.

Late one evening after I had signed off, there was a loud thump, and then someone said the name of one of my daughters. The following morning my daughter and I returned to the tape recorder, and she asked if anyone had a message for her. Thelma, a friend of my daughter's who had been killed several years ago, said her name clearly. My daughter asked Thelma whether she had a message, and Thelma replied, *"I want to,"* twice during the recording and once just as it ended. There was no further message.

The next two messages are interesting.

One evening as I ended recording for the day, a male voice uttered in fast tempo, *"You're looking pretty."*

How nice! I thought, and went happily to bed.

The following morning I made three recordings, receiving a number of firm, clear Class A messages; however, nothing was heard from my admirer of the evening before.

That evening I made one recording. At 9:55 I had signed off when a female voice of unusual quality and rhythm, similar to that heard the evening before said, *"I'm looking pretty."*

I had to conclude the message the evening before was not intended for me, but for this unknown female entity who had taken twenty-three hours to reply. We saw the same thing with the Paul White recordings, and here we have it again; this is another example of how time must be different in the next dimension from our own. The female voice, sounding pleased with herself, acted as if *"You're looking pretty"* had just been said. For us it was twenty-three hours later, but she gave every indication it had been only a moment to her.

It is my practice to give instant feedback about the messages I have recorded. In this way I leave no doubt in the minds of those who speak about what I have been able to pick up from them and what I haven't. That was exactly what I did one evening: I repeated the messages from the previous taping to them and then signed off. The *"Yes, recorded"* message seemed their acknowledgment to one another of what I had received from their communications.

I had expressed disappointment one evening over having difficulty getting loud, clear voices for several days. As I reached to turn off the tape recorder a hurt voice said *"We try to give help!"* in unusually clear quality.

Twelve hours after receiving in slow, accented rhythm, *"This drum it seems to fail,"* I asked what they had meant. The answer came back: *"It's improved again."* This voice had unusual quality and was loud and clear. Several counters later the voice heard the evening before came in with, *"We fail with coppia."* I still have no idea what either meant but suspect this information referred to their recording and transmitting equipment. Because of their nature and the repeated use of the word *"fail,"* I tend to conclude the two messages are related.

The *"La bravé great salesman. Bigs bra bravit"* polyglot message came from my French friend in the spirit world. He spoke to me first in Maryland and then followed me to New Jersey. The French dictionary reveals several definitions for *"bravé"* (good, honest, brave). He may have been telling me, since I had been asking who he was, that he is an honest, great salesman. The second part of the message, which came five counters after the first, has not been so easy to translate. Since I have no knowledge of French, I had to write everything phonetically as it was received, and so therein may lie the difficulty. *"Bras"* in French can mean power, action, assistance. *"Bravit"* seems related to the word *"brav"* used in the first sentence. Breaking it all down, and permitting my imagination to leap about, perhaps he was saying that he, an honest salesman, was going to give me big, brave help!

"We really like you. You're very pretty. We count you" all came within six counters on the tape recorder and were said by the same individual.

Twenty-four hours later I referred back to this message and asked what they had meant by, *"We count you."* The same voice as heard the day before shouted, *"I like you! I'm by you."* In the next recording I asked if he meant by this that he was in my office. *"That's right,"* he said.

I had been experimenting, trying to find the best way for the voices to come through. As I signed off one morning I told them, since they seemed to speak more clearly when I used the air-band on my radio as a background sound source, I would use that method. A slow, deliberate voice said, *"That's much better. Yes, it will help me."*

"Gut night," seems to have been an unknown German friend replying to my own "Good night!"

A message came through one day that helped me understand a message Styhe had given several months earlier. At the time, although I had said nothing, I hadn't known what Styhe meant. This morning I did, so at the end of the recording I told him now I knew the meaning of his earlier message. With this the message, *"We treasure her,"* was recorded.

One morning in September I ended recording early because I had to attend a meeting. I explained at the end of the second recording the reason I had to stop. Someone asked, *"Where you going?"* He evidently was aware of my preparations to leave but had not heard the explanation.

As mentioned, Margo usually says just her name. One evening, though, she said, *"Take a walk after ten,"* followed by her name. I wasn't sure whether she was suggesting I take a walk or telling me this is what she did.

The following morning, wanting to make sure the message had come from her, I asked if she had said this ten hours earlier. *"Oh, yes!"* she answered. In the second recording that morning I asked if she wanted me to take a walk, and in accented rhythm she replied, *"Yes, I do."* I tried to find out her reason for this, but nothing further came through.

Until the spirit photography session with the medium, my own picture-taking attempts of my spirit friends all met with failure. The following incident is an example of this.

I had signed off late one evening, and a female voice, sounding as if she were standing at my elbow, said, *"Take a portrait!"* Before she could change her mind, I grabbed my Polaroid from the top of the file cabinet a few feet away. Where should I aim it? I wondered. Trying to take a picture of someone you can't see is a strange sensation. Finally I suggested she position herself in front of a white magnetic board in my office. Not knowing how long it might take her to do this, I waited for a few seconds, and then, hoping for the best, said, "All right now. I'm going to snap the shutter." When the photo developed, there was nothing standing before the magnetic board.

The following morning I told my unseen friend I was sorry, but I had been unable to get her portrait.

Sounding as if she were still at my elbow and the failure was all my fault, she replied, *"I come'd here!"*

When I sign off at night, those on the other side frequently say, *"Good night!"* In the TV special about my work, I am shown at the end of the program sitting at my tape recorder saying, "Thank you again for being here this evening, and good night." In less than three seconds a clear paranormal voice replied, *"Good night!"*

Thus far, the voices from beyond have shared with us their thoughts and experiences in many areas. They have spoken about death and dying. They have given us glimpses of their world and their lives. They have demonstrated their clairaudient, clairvoyant, and precognitive abilities. They have answered some of our questions about reincarnation and a number of other areas.

There is a theory that we have two bodies, a physical as well as an etheric body, which is the double of the physical. At death the etheric body separates from the physical and moves on to the next dimension. I asked if this was a correct belief, and a clear voice answered, *"True."*

The following day during my recording I discussed the matter of the silver cord that supposedly attaches the etheric body to the physical. It is this cord so the theory goes that permits out-of-body travel to any place in the world, or even to other worlds. As long as the silver cord remains attached to the physical body, no harm will come to one. When out-of-body travel is over, this cord brings the two bodies safely back together. At death the silver cord, we are told, breaks and permits the etheric body to float free. My question as to whether the silver cord is broken at that time was answered with, *"You're right."* During the same recording I asked if the breaking of the silver cord was what permitted a person to move into the spirit world. Someone said several times, *"That is right."*

Last spring I was exploring the question of other worlds and dimensions with my spirit friends. My question about how many dimensions there are brought the Class A answer, *"You should ask Swann."* They were evidently referring to Ingo Swann of California, a noted psychic, who has frequently demonstrated under controlled laboratory conditions the ability to have out-of-body experiences. This is a good example of how those on the other side are aware of our efforts.

Some individuals who don't deny that strange manifestations seem to take place in and around so-called haunted houses are still skeptical in attributing this condition to ghosts. Instead, they allege that we leave behind a psychic imprint when we die and that these imprints can occasionally affect matter.

In Chapter 7 I mentioned the contact I had with the ghosts who seem to inhabit the Edgar Allan Poe house in Baltimore; I also discussed trips to Point Lookout State Park in southern Maryland. Both of these locations, I feel, have much more to them than psychic imprints. Remember how an unseen entity told me, when I asked about the extraneous voices on the Poe tape: *"They work there in their place. They were in their house today."* We must also not forget the interaction that took place between some of the ghosts and those of us visiting the lighthouse at Point Lookout. The ghosts made independent comments of their own, on tape, as we were walking through the lighthouse. They showed an awareness of us, and of what we were saying. Their remarks were pertinent to the situation existing at that moment, and were not caused by a psychic imprint carried over from a hundred years earlier.

I have further explored through my tape recorder whether unexplained manifestations at haunted locations are the result of conscious intervention by discarnate entities. A number of provocative answers have been returned. The first message taped was a clear voice pleading, *"Make me free."* With this message I had to wonder if I was again being put in touch with an actual situation I had asked about, and if the *"Make me free"* entity was a ghost.

During the same recording when I asked if there were ghosts, someone replied, *"Right!"* Later when I asked if conscious entities who were involved in hauntings might wish, at times, to be set free to move on into the spirit world, four Class A answers came back: *"Right!" "That's right." "Pick it up, Estep." "That's right."*

After playing this segment of tape and hearing the answers, I repeated to the entities, as is my custom, what I had recorded about ghosts. Still in a Class A voice, an entity commented, *"You did."*

Three days after this, when I asked whether ghosts who haunt locations are always aware of doing this, someone told me, *"Yes, I do."*

Not realizing this had been said, I went on to add that at times it seems ghosts think they are still earth-plane personalities. *"That's right"* came back twice.

I then queried why individuals wouldn't know they died, and the puzzling answer *"Because we have a split house"* was returned. One counter later someone agreed with this comment and said, *"That's right."* A moment later a final answer came back: *"I couldn't forget her."*

This last answer seems to explain why at least one ghost refused to move on to the spirit world. There was apparently a woman he couldn't forget, and he wanted to stay here. We remember how the ghost Howie, at Point Lookout, told me, *"I don't think of her."* When I heard this on tape, I wondered whether Howie was trying to convince himself or me about the matter.

One month after the *"Make me free"* message was recorded I turned the microphone over to those on the other side, inviting them to ask me any questions they wished. A clear voice said, *"Let Joy."*

In the second recording I told Joy I had recorded her name, and if she would like to ask me a question, I would try to answer it. Almost immediately she answered, *"You can't set me free."*

On playback I realized she sounded like the person I had heard from a month earlier. During the third recording I asked if she was the individual who'd said *"Make me free"*; she replied, *"I is."*

During the next two days I called upon Joy several times and tried to give her suggestions as to what she could do if she wanted to leave the earth plane. Although answers came back, I couldn't be positive they were coming from Joy. At one point she seemed to say, *"Help him. I love him."* Like the male entity who indicated he hadn't moved to the spirit world because of a woman he wanted to stay with, perhaps Joy had a similar reason for remaining behind.

Last spring I brought up the subject of materialization for the first time with those on the other side. We also discussed frequency and vibration.

When I asked why they didn't materialize more often so we

could see them, someone replied in an echo effect, *"We try to."* During the same recording I asked if it was difficult for them to do this. *"It isn't easy,"* I was told.

I asked if they were able to materialize by merely slowing down their vibrations and frequency. *"Certainly not!"* was the response.

In July I taped, *"I was here. I was here last night."*

In the next recording I inquired who was here. An unknown entity replied, *"Adam Kusick."* I then asked if the person who'd spoken in the first recording had tried to materialize the night before. *"I did. That's right"* was taped.

There is no longer any doubt in my mind that many unseen friends, like Adam, enter my office during recordings.

On the first of August, someone said to me in a loud voice sounding nearby, *"You seated them."* This may have referred to my customary invitation as I start to record: I tell the spirits all of them are welcome who come in friendship and peace.

Once when I began to record, after waiting for those who wished to to join me, I was told, *"They're still not here."*

Near the end of August a voice said, *"We come now"* and five counters later, *"I'm sitting on your right."*

Three days after this I reviewed a message Styhe had given me earlier in which he'd said if I wanted him to speak, I should call on him first. I asked why I should do this, and he replied, *"We don't want anybody to stay by your chair."* I inferred from this that it would be more difficult for him to communicate if there were others around me.

The next day I asked if my friends waited before coming and standing by me until the individual I had first called upon spoke. In one of the loudest and clearest voices I have on file, a voice replied, *"That's correct!"*

In September, when I asked where my friends were, I was told, *"They're next to you."*

During recording the morning of October fifteenth I asked if it was necessary to have spirit friends with me in my office in order to record voices. Someone said, *"You don't have any there now."* I asked where they sat. Within a few seconds a voice answered, running some of the words together, *"You asked me the other time who sits right by beside you."* This could have been true, because in each recording I ask who is with me.

Not knowing these two messages had come through, I went on to ask if they were sitting on the chairs in my office. Someone replied in a Class A singing mode, *"Look round about you."*

In November, when I asked where my friends were, an unusually clear male voice sounded nearby: *"At the clock, Vicky and Papa."* There is a wall clock next to the window in my office, so that was apparently where they were.

Four months later, while I was packing, preparing to move to a new house, I came across a book I had purchased a year before in a secondhand bookstore entitled *The Girl from Alsace* by Burton E. Stevenson. It was in deplorable condition—moldy, pages crinkled from dampness, spine broken. I wondered why I had bought it. Looking inside, I saw the reason. It had been a gift; in fact, it seemed as if it had been two gifts. Such books have a special poignancy for me.

This is what I read: "Xmas 1918. To Papa from Marie." Down at the bottom of the page were the additional words "To Scott from Paul and Vicky." The old-fashioned handwriting was similar, suggesting that the book may have gone from one member of the same family to another. All the handwriting was cursive, except for Vicky's. She had printed her name in a careful but childish scrawl.

What of Papa and Vicky on tape who came one day to observe the recording? Could they be the same, or was it merely coincidence? Although I find it increasingly difficult to accept events as coincidental, I won't go so far as to say coincidences never happen. Still, the name Papa is not often used today, and Vicky is not the most common name for females. I decided to attempt to contact them the following day.

At the beginning of this March recording, I asked those on the other side to try to bring me Vicky and Papa who had been by the clock in my office in November. Someone answered, *"They can speak."* Later I asked if they were the same individuals whose names were written in the book I had bought. A clear male voice replied, *"Yes, we are the same"* and six counters later added in a loud voice, *"That's right."*

All of this opens so many questions for consideration, it is difficult to know where to begin. While it is true that I had felt a rush of sadness for the individuals whose names were written in the book when I bought it, the emotional involvement was brief—so brief, I had forgotten all about it until I came across the book as I was getting ready to move.

Nevertheless, there was obviously enough attraction to cause Papa and Vicky to join me in my office in November and to return in March when I asked them to try to come through again.

What is it? What do we and those on the other side have that draws us together in such an unexplainable way?

Many favor an electromagnetic explanation, and they may be right. Could it have been that the book in my office acted as a magnet and drew these two entities to my side last November? Or was it the empathy I felt as I stood in a bookstore a year ago, my mind reaching out for these five unknown individuals, wondering for a moment what their fate had been? Perhaps it was both. Whatever the answer or answers, it seems we are closely tied, one to the other, in life as well as in death.

In their tape-recorded messages those in the next dimension have exhibited a keen awareness of us on the earth plane, as well as a willingness and an eagerness to share with us what takes place in their own world.

Chapter 11—
Communications
from the Well-
Known

> Souls which once were in men, when they leave the
> body, need not cease from benefiting mankind.
> Some indeed, in addition to other services, give
> occult messages, thus proving by their own case
> that other souls also survive. —Plotinus

During all my years of taping I have made it a firm practice
not to call on the famous or infamous. If I were to call on Julius
Caesar, and a bright, happy voice replied, *"Here I am,"* how
could I know it was really Caesar? I couldn't, and to think otherwise would be the height of delusion. I leave the notables
strictly alone. If some well-known personality speaks to me
from the other side, my first thought is, "It can't be," and then,
wanting to be at least fair, I say "Prove it." This, obviously,
considering that I communicate by tape recorder, is usually difficult. Now and then, however, additional messages and evidence are received that cause me to stop and give further thought
to whether these personalities are who they claim to be.

"You have the famous Beethoven" was taped early one
morning in September when I asked if I had friends present.

Beethoven? Surely not. I decided it must be someone on the
other side trying to catch my attention. I was busy packing in
preparation to leave my summer home in New Jersey and move
back to Maryland. It was during the last recording before putting

the tape recorder in its box that the Beethoven message had come through.

That afternoon while driving home, I had over three hours to give Beethoven, and the taped voices in general, some thought.

I still doubted that the message, although it was very clear and without question an electronic voice, was truly from Beethoven. At the same time I remembered various musical notes and chords I had received over the years that I was convinced originated in another dimension. These musical notes had grown more frequent since the death of my mother thirteen months earlier. I also recalled questions I had asked about musicians and music in the spirit world and their responses—that they had pianos in their world and continued to play music to *"share with their brothers."*

At the age of five I began taking piano lessons from my mother, who was a church organist for over fifty years. From an early age, I have loved classical music. In my early teens I started pipe organ lessons and played the organ for various churches in Pennsylvania and Maryland. My grounding in music is good and reasonably thorough. I continued to study music in college, including musical composition. Could my affinity for music and my message from the purported *"famous Beethoven"* possibly be another case of some sort of empathy between an individual on the other side and myself?

Rosemary Brown of England, mentioned in Chapter 2, has played hundreds of compositions she believes were channeled through her by famous musicians who have died. Beethoven is one of the composers she feels has dictated music to her.

It seems reasonable to me that those seeking to prove their after-death existence will do this in different ways and often to different people. Could Beethoven possibly be attempting this, not only by channeling music through Mrs. Brown, but by having someone tell me, through my tape recorder, of his presence? It was doubtful, though not impossible, and certainly if nothing further was heard from the good maestro, I could dismiss it as an interesting aberration.

The morning after the Beethoven message I was back in my office with my tape recorder. I asked if Beethoven had been with me the day before. *"That's so. Yes, that was correct"* came the answer. As I ended the recording I told Beethoven I hoped he would come back many times. *"I shall!"* was the Class A reply.

Later, considering the two messages, I felt there was nothing evidential about either of them. Any male spirit voice could have spoken. The following morning, when I started my taping and asked if I had friends present, a Class A male voice replied, *"Ludwig."* Not knowing this had been received, I went on to ask Beethoven if he was with me. *"I am,"* answered the same voice. Continuing, I inquired whether he thought he could play some music for me. *"Yes, I can. I can."* This was immediately followed with a musical chord and several musical notes, and then the message, *"Yes, that's it!"*

After playing this recording back and hearing the messages, and especially the music, I started to consider seriously that I might be hearing from Beethoven.

I made another recording and asked if the music had come from him. Still Class A, a male voice answered, *"You can say, say, that came from,"* and a moment later, *"That can come to the same."*

On the morning of September 12 several additional messages were received, apparently from Beethoven, in which he said he would try to play for me that night. I expressed joy at hearing this and said I would return to my tape recorder in the evening in the hope he could bring music through. Still, searching for evidence that I was in communication with him, I suggested he try to play part of his "Ode to Joy" for me. "If you do this," I said, "I'll have proof I'm hearing from you."

That night there was a severe electrical storm. The electricity flickered off several times, and I delayed going to my tape recorder. I have a healthy respect for lightning and stay away from the recorder and other electronic equipment in my office during a storm. I almost didn't go this time. There was a compulsion, however, to make the recording. I had told Beethoven, or whomever, I would be there, so I went. Turning on my tape recorder, with thunder rolling in the background and lightning flashing all around me, I knew this would be a short recording. I was here, as I had promised. If nothing was heard within several minutes, that would be it. Everything on the voices' end of the line was quiet. Enough! I thanked Beethoven for any effort he might have made to come through, and as I reached to turn off the recorder, soft music, at first tentative, started to come through the speaker of my radio which was set on the air-band and which I was using as a sound source. I sat back amazed. The music, which lasted for a minute, was clear and grew in strength. There were bells and the sound of wind, along with several instruments playing simultaneously that I couldn't identify. The thunder still crashed in the background. A certain amount of crackling in the radio from nearby lightning affected the sound but I had little doubt I was recording music from another dimension. It was an extremely moving occasion. I felt greatly blessed to be the recipient of such a gift.

At the conclusion of the music several voices, in answer to my query as to whether the music was coming from the spirit world said, *"That's right."* A few seconds later, a loud, strongly rhythmic, and very pleased male voice added, *"We are good!"*

My attempt to discover what this music was did not end on the evening of September 12. Although I was convinced the music had originated in another reality, I wanted to remove as much doubt as possible. I duplicated it onto cassette tapes and sent it to the music departments of the local high school and nearby college. Not wanting to predispose their judgment either for or against the possible paranormal origins of the music, I asked only if anyone could identify it for me. No one could. I next sent it to six well-known musicians, all listed in *Who's Who*, with whom I'd had contact in the past. With them I fully explained the situation and in addition sent a tape of all the contacts I had from or about Beethoven. Different comments came back indicating they found it fascinating, unusual music, but each admitted he was unable to identify it. David Ohanian of the Boston Symphony and Pops replied, "The intervals involved could not have been harmonized in conventional manner and make sense." Donald Martino, Chairman of the Department of Composition, New England Conservatory of Music, awarded the Pulitzer prize for music in 1974, wrote that he and his colleagues had listened to it a number of times, but no one had heard the music before. Without exception, each musician who replied said that it did not sound like the music Beethoven had composed while living. This is true, but Beethoven has been dead for over 160 years and cannot be expected to compose the same type of music he did almost 200 years ago.

Recently I replayed the music for the first time in over a year. I was suddenly struck with the realization that twenty seconds after the music begins, there is a two-measure segment that sounds like a piano and is very similar to two measures near the beginning of the first movement of Beethoven's Opus 27, No. 2, better known as "Moonlight Sonata." I had my daughter play the two measures from the "Moonlight Sonata" on the piano while I sat beside her and played the two measures of the tape-recorded music from the next dimension. They sounded almost identical.

After the outstanding efforts made by Beethoven and his friends to bring the music through, and one can only imagine the tremendous difficulties they must have encountered to do this, my contacts with him did not cease. They continued for some time, and on two occasions faint music was heard.

One evening, when I asked if Beethoven was standing by, I heard the soft notes of a scale being played in the background. A young boy's voice then clearly sang, *"Pick it up. Yes, he is. Up."* Although the singing was not done in the true scale heard on the tape, it is partly sung on the scale. It is also interesting that the seven-word message compares with seven notes heard in a diatonic scale.

Other messages were received, now and then, including the name *"Ludwig"* in two instances.

What can one say about the Beethoven communications? Are they genuine? The evidence strongly points to the validity of the contact. Beethoven had a firm belief that mankind survives death and is apparently trying to show us this, first, evidently through Rosemary Brown, and now, perhaps perceiving that many people are skeptical of Mrs. Brown's channeling, he is trying to show us this more strongly by tape.

Although Beethoven did not play any part of his "Ode to Joy" as I had requested the morning of September 12, he chose to include two measures from his Opus 27 as his musical signature. By so doing, he shows that he is still continuing his life of music in a fully conscious state in another reality.

Five months before I first heard from Beethoven, I learned that another personality who had spoken to me a number of times was more famous than I had thought. As mentioned earlier, I had frequently taped messages from an entity called James, but my attempts to learn his last name brought only the reply *"James."*

There were several interesting facets to the James personality. He seemed to stay with me, instead of speaking a time or two as many spirit communicators do before continuing on their way, never to be heard from again. Almost every time I called on him, he would indicate his presence. He also seemed unusually good at bringing me to those with whom I wished to speak. James was so obliging in this, I called him my unofficial gatekeeper. Not wanting to use him just in this capacity, if he wished otherwise, I would occasionally ask him a question or turn the microphone over to him if he had a special message. Normally I wouldn't hear anything back, but sometimes he would speak, and I began to get the impression there was more to James than I had originally believed.

Somewhat belatedly, it occurred to me that James might be the last name of the entity who spoke. After additional thought I wondered if he could possibly be William James.

I knew very little about the noted William James except that he had been interested in psychical research before his death. In a college psychology course I remembered having read that he was a famous psychologist and educator who had died in the early 1900s.

One evening, sitting down at my tape recorder, I asked, "James, are you the William James who was a psychologist and educator?"

I was quickly put in my place by a clear female voice who told me, *"William James is a noted philosophist."*

"Philosophist" was obviously related to philosophy, so I went to my encyclopedia and looked up William James. From there I learned that James was a psychologist and educator, as I already knew, whose outstanding work had been done in philosophy, and it was in that field he had wanted to be especially remembered.

The next morning, when I asked James if he was the well-known psychologist and philosopher who died in the early 1900s, a male voice replied, *"You're right."* During this same recording I asked if he had been surprised at what he'd found upon reaching the spirit world. The same male voice from a moment earlier answered, *"Yes. Come, you're with Polly. Your Polly's here."* James also said he would help me.

I have been unable to learn whether James was close to a "Polly" in his earth-plane life, but evidently he knew someone by that name and met her after death.

The following day I asked if he would really help me. Very

clearly, the voice heard the previous day said, *"I will help you. I'll do that. Right. Sally. You see, I experienced hate. And we help. We help you."* This was followed by a different voice asking *"We help her?"* and the reply *"Yes."*

From then on I stopped using James as my gatekeeper and asked him questions pointed more in the direction of philosophy and psychical research. I deliberately avoided reading any biographies about him; I wanted my questions, and his answers, to remain as "pure" as possible without being influenced by knowledge gained through a written biography. I hoped to be able to get a better feel for this man, and then later I would read a biography and see if anything evidential had come out of our contacts.

Months of frequent communications followed. Many of my questions were answered by a male voice sounding like his. He was the individual who once, when I asked if he was standing by, replied with, *"The faithful still have it,"* indicating he was one of the faithful. On another occasion I asked where other realities existed, and he answered, *"That's really not important."* Three weeks later I asked him if he had his choice, where he would choose to live—the spirit world or the earth plane; he responded, *"We don't worry about that."* My question about how much free will an individual had on the earth plane as well as in the spirit world brought the reply *"A great deal."* Eleven days later when I called on him, someone asked the interesting question, *"Will the item speak?"* This was followed by James's answer, *"I will be. Thank you. James."* Two days after this, when I again called on James, a clear voice declared, *"He's taking a walk,"* and repeated it a moment later.

When I finally borrowed a biography about William James from the library, I learned that one of his chief pleasures had been taking long walks. I also learned that James's health had not been robust and that he would work to the point of exhaustion. At times James's voice would become weak, as if it were almost too difficult for him to speak. I once asked him about this, and he affirmed that he wasn't feeling well. A few days later I asked if he had seen a doctor; he replied that he had. In the next recording when I asked what the doctor had said, he answered, *"Too tired. Work."* A week later I was talking to James and reminded him he'd said he'd been tired, when he interrupted: *"I still am."* Not knowing this had been taped, I went on to inquire if he felt better. A different voice explained, *"She ask if you feel good."*

One of James's beliefs had been that man not only needed God but that God needed man. I asked him if he still felt that way, and somewhat excitedly he said, *"Yes, that's it! Yes, you can say that."*

Another time when I asked him if consciousness, which differs with each individual, is the only reality, he replied clearly, *"Merely cognive."*

Since he was so involved in psychical research I also tried to explore this area with him but without much success. My question to him about what he thought today's psychical researchers should concentrate on was dismissed somewhat irritably with *"Come. Come, come, come. Some other problem."*

Comparing the James and Beethoven communications, I am impressed with how different they are. The James biography pointed out that he was extremely interested in the question of postmortem survival. He tried, in many ways, to prove to himself that humans survived death, but the issue was never resolved to his satisfaction. Now, on the other side, knowing postmortem survival as fact, he is attempting to show us, by his own example, how we continue to live after the death of the physical body.

James's remark about "white crows" is famous in survival literature. He said it required only one white crow to prove that not all crows are black. He implied by this that if we could prove even one human being survived death, then we might begin to accept that survival is available for all. He appears to be trying to do this, even more so than Beethoven, by coming through to many different people in various ways. Indeed, many people claim to have had contact with him "beyond the veil." Susy Smith felt James had channeled her book, *The Book of James*, published in 1974, through her. Four years later Jane Roberts wrote *The Afterdeath Journal of an American Philosopher—The World View of William James*; this was another case of apparent channeling. Groups that meet for enlightenment claim James and his associates come through to try to enlighten them.

Are all these contacts genuine? No one can truly say, but I suspect at least some of them are. Considering William James's background it is not surprising that he might be trying to prove that his white crow has become a flock.

I found James to be somewhat testy at times. Beethoven never was. Always, with James, I was like a student with a respected professor. I experienced a certain amount of awe during the moments I was communicating with Beethoven, and yet, in a strange way, I felt more in partnership with him than I did with James. Both men, giants in their fields, are continuing to pursue their same interests after death; both are endeavoring to let us know we can do the same when it becomes our time to return to the world beyond death.

There have been other contacts, in most cases brief, never initiated by me, with or about the famous, and in one case, the infamous.

The infamous one came during a recording the morning of May 11. All messages were on the reverse or wrong side of the tape. Those in other dimensions speak to us on both sides of our recording tapes. We will go into this thoroughly in Chapter 18.

As I played the tape back I heard, within a span of about four minutes, four Class A messages. The first was, *"Show me no evil."* A different voice followed with, *"I brought him in."* Next was heard, *"He's coward,"* and the final message in the group was, *"I got Hitler. He dreams I bring his mother."*

Since recording those four messages, I have read that Hitler was unusually fond of his mother.

Over a period of five months I seemed to be surrounded by scientists. They would drop into my office, at times speak to me personally, and then after several visits continue on their way.

In October I taped, *"Eddington."* For the next week I tried to find out who was on the tape. Being largely unsuccessful, I don't know if I had Sir Arthur Eddington, the English astronomer, physicist, and writer interested in psychical research, on tape or not. Eddington spoke on both sides of my tape, and once someone said he had brought four others with him. Eight days after recording the name *"Eddington"* for the first time, I again asked if he was present. On the reverse side of the tape an unusually clear Class A male voice answered, *"That's still my name, but I wish she'd never heard. I rest!"*

I feel the voice may well have been that of Sir Arthur Eddington, since he came at the start of the scientists' period. I believe he was interested in what I was doing but wasn't eager for me to be aware of it and found my calling on him bothersome. After taping the message *". . . I wish she'd never heard . . ."* I apologized for disturbing him and assured him I wouldn't call on him again. I feel when entities on the other side show they don't welcome being contacted, one must respect their wish for privacy.

A somewhat different situation arose with Darwin (presumably Charles). Early one morning I taped, *"Yes, it is. Guess he now is Darwin."* A few days later someone excitedly told me, *"You got a scientist in the room!"* Five months after this I taped *"I'm around here, Darwin,"* followed by, *"If I need help, I see a laser around it."* All the Darwin messages were good Class A and came through on the reverse side of my recording tape.

On the morning of October 6, 1981 I was eating breakfast while listening to the news on the radio, as I do each morning. The lead-off announcement was that President Anwar Sadat had been shot while reviewing a parade in Cairo. The announcer reported that although he had been rushed to the hospital, his wound did not appear serious.

Later that morning I made my usual ten-minute recording. After replaying the tape in the forward mode, I turned it over and played it in reverse. Almost immediately I heard, *"May the God give off,"* followed several counters later with, *"God the giver. God the giver."* The voice sounded familiar and was so powerful and clear, I stopped playback, as I wondered who it might be. My first thought was it sounded like Sadat, but the radio announcer had reassured us that he had not been seriously wounded. Whoever it was seemed to be having a death experience. *"May the God give off,"* I interpreted as his asking God to have mercy on him. The following message indicated to me that the person had received God's mercy when he said, *"God the giver. God the giver."*

I pushed the play button to see if there was anything further on the tape. Within a minute a different male voice said, *"Sadazi. He is here,"* with, one counter later, *"I'm back."* The use of the word *"Sadazi"* is perhaps strange but certainly close enough to Sadat that we can accept it was he to whom it referred.

Was Sadat dead? I turned on my radio, and with the next news broadcast learned he had in fact died from his wounds.

The following day when I inquired about Sadat, someone

spoke on the reverse side of the tape and said, *"Sadat greatness."*

I had long admired President Sadat and what he tried to do for Egypt and its masses of poverty-stricken people. Perhaps it was this sympathy for him that allowed me to tune in to his death experience. Whatever the reason, I felt greatly privileged and humbled to be there as a silent observer.

Less than one percent of my total communications have come from the well-known. Although I would advise caution about accepting at face value messages from those who claim to have been famous, I nevertheless think it a disservice to categorically rule them out. If Uncle Joe and Aunt Susy and Tom and Mary make an effort to speak to us, why forbid Beethoven and James and the others from doing the same? I would consider the background of any well-known personality who gives his or her name. Wherever possible, I ask for proof, as I did with Beethoven. He supplied this in a far greater way than I ever dreamed.

Chapter 12—Voices from Egypt

Egypt has called to me for years. In 1984, when I finally visited the "Land of the Nile," the visible and invisible spoke to me in many ways. As soon as I saw the three pyramids of Giza standing like sentinels in the full moonlight, I knew I was where I belonged. That feeling never left during the two weeks I was there.

Six months earlier I had learned that a group of nineteen people, led by Lynn Gardner of Indianapolis, Indiana, would be visiting Egypt in May. The focus of the trip was to explore not only the past and present civilizations of Egypt, but to attempt to reach other realities through song, dance, meditation, and whatever way seemed right to each particular individual. In my own case I hoped to record voices from other dimensions through a tape recorder.

During my years of taping, the spirit voices have usually reached me through a recorder located in the office of my home. It is one thing to record messages from the other side in the comfort of your home using modern equipment; however, trying to achieve contact with other realms for days at a time under the rugged, primitive conditions found in many parts of Egypt is something very different.

Once I had decided to go on this journey, I began assembling all I would need. Because my daughter Becky was going along and had agreed to try some recordings on her own, I knew we would require additional equipment. All our recordings were to be done with batteries. Convenient electrical outlets are not found in 4,000-year-old tombs carved from rock. Both tape recorders used AA batteries, and I bought forty, thinking this would be sufficient. (It wasn't, but additional batteries were found at many locations for one dollar each.) I stuck with sixty-minute tapes, because longer tapes in portable tape recorders have given me problems in the past. We brought fifty hours worth of tapes, and that was more than enough. Several small, powerful pocket flashlights were included so we could see what we were doing in the dark tombs and know when a tape had come to an end and needed to be changed. I had a horror of taping over something already taped, but fortunately that never happened. A small, inexpensive battery checker was one of the most important tools I took. Each morning, before leaving the hotel for the day, I checked batteries in both tape recorders. If they proved less than perfect, they were changed. Several lead laminated pouches specifically designed to protect film against airport X ray damage held some of our film as well as some tapes. They, along with the forty batteries and the rest of the tapes, fit into my carry-on case. Even so, I had the bag hand-checked at each airport security gate. The guards were gracious about this despite a few raised eyebrows at the sight of so many tapes and batteries.

Our group assembled at Kennedy Airport in New York. Shortly thereafter we were aboard a Royal Jordanian airliner for our flight to Amman. From there we transferred to Egyptian Air for a short hop to Cairo. Security was tight. In Amman all the men were frisked before being permitted to board the plane for Egypt. When we landed in Cairo, our plane was met by a soldier in full battle dress cradling a rifle.

Later as I stood by the window of my hotel room in Giza and saw the pyramids just a short distance away, I was filled with awe. I wondered what the outcome of my quest would be. Over the years I have learned that the invisibles can communicate with us on tape, but would this ability to speak extend to the inside of ancient tombs and temples? Might ongoing consciousness still remain there? If consciousness was found in such places, what would its nature be? Would I be communicating with 4,000-year-old earthbound entities, or would conscious entities from the higher realms, who might or might not have played a historical part in the locations where I would record, agree to speak to me through something as prosaic as a tape recorder?

Some of my questions were answered the first day I recorded. Our tour bus had taken us to Memphis, the capital of the Old Kingdom of Lower Egypt, to see the famous alabaster sphinx and a colossal statue of Ramses II. On the palm-shaded grounds lay an open sarcophagus. Holding my recorder inside the sarcophagus I gave the invitation for someone to speak. When I played that segment of tape back later in the bus, I heard a clear male voice say, *"Need help!"* During the morning we also visited the area around the step pyramid of Zoser and entered several mastabas (long, flat tomb buildings) and temples. Additional messages, some very loud and clear, were received. In one tomb, after I put the recorder into what the early Egyptians called the "false door," a clear male voice sang, *"I'm coming down."*

Physical stamina was severly tested at times, especially the afternoon some of us climbed the cliffs to the rock tombs of Beni Hassan. The thirty-nine tombs, cut out of rock, were used largely by local rulers of the Middle Kingdom and date back to 2,000 B.C. We first crossed the Nile by ferryboat, then rode donkeys to the cliffs. A very steep climb followed, leaving us exhausted. As soon as I caught my breath, I moved around quietly in the tomb of Khiti, inviting the unseen to speak. Several did, but the most interesting message came after I asked them who they were. A female voice, evidently speaking to others in her world, said, *"Come in and think of what you are."* It appears that, at least in that particular group, although a type of consciousness exists, no one has self-labeled oneself as we do in our world.

In the five Beni Hassan tombs we visited twelve messages were received. During the twelve days I recorded in Egypt, I began each recording with "We are seekers of the light. We come to you in love and truth, and we ask you to do the same." An unusually large number of messages received at Beni Hassan, and at other locations, assured me they also came in love and truth, evidence that they heard my actual words and could respond in kind.

It was at the Bagit tomb of Beni Hassan that my own name was first recorded in Egypt. One voice said, *"With her. Estep say,"* and a moment later, *"Estep call."* It was also at the Bagit tomb that someone gave me a precognitive message.

Taking pictures in many tombs is strictly prohibited because the flash of cameras can further fade the beautiful painted murals. The tombs of Beni Hassan were no exception, and the guard followed our group closely, making sure the rule was observed. I was standing in a small alcove of the Bagit tomb talking into my recorder when the guard, thinking the black object I held in my hand was a camera, started over to me with stick threateningly upraised. I speak no Arabic, and he spoke no English, so it looked like we were about to have an unpleasant incident. All I could do was hold my tape recorder in front of me and show by smiles and gestures it was not a camera I held but a tape recorder for recording words. After a moment the guard seemed to understand. He lowered his stick, smiled, and walked away so I was free to continue recording. On tape playback later that evening I heard a clear male voice say less than a minute before the incident, *"Have no fear."*

The morning of the ninth day we visited the Temple of Abydos, which was the chief center of the cult of Osiris. It is here that Becky, while sitting alone in a small sanctuary, recorded the most beautiful, unusual paranormal singing I have heard. Most of it is in an unknown tongue, and I suspect it is no language known to us on the earth plane. A small part of it, however, was in English. It begins with, *"We are loving."*

It was at Abydos that I also received a special message. At the conclusion of each recording in Egypt I always said, "We leave you with love. We ask for your blessing." A few seconds after I ended an Abydos recording an excellent Class A voice replied, *"Got your blessing!"*

That afternoon we moved on to the Temple of Dendera, dedicated to Hathor, the goddess of love and beauty. There are a number of chambers in the temple as well as bats. Everywhere you look you can see them clinging to the ceiling and swooping madly from one room to the next. Praying that their radar systems were in good working order and that none were rabid, I clung to a metal ladder that would take me deep into the earth under the temple. It was here in a small room that secret magical ceremonies had been performed thousands of years ago, and I sensed it would be a good place for recording voices. Few people had ventured down there, so I had enough physical room, yet I felt crowded. It was as if the energies existing there over the centuries had become compacted, and pushed against anything that entered. I made one brief recording lasting about three minutes. The first message received was a loud, shrill female voice saying, *"We come."* At the end of the recording an outstanding loud, clear male voice called me by name: *"Sarah. Please guide me. I love."*

Out of more than a dozen locations where voices were recorded, the two places that affected me the most were a group of Coptic Christian tombs in the Western desert and a small, seldom-visited tomb close to the pyramids.

After completing a special ceremony in the area of the pyramids, a guide took us to a tomb dating back thousands of years. The lights were turned off so we could meditate, but not before I saw a statue of a young boy possibly twelve to fourteen years of age in a small wall niche. Immediately I was overcome with the greatest sense of loss and desolation I have ever felt. For a time I was unable to speak, my feeling of grief was so intense. During this time my tape recorder was recording as I sat on the floor under his statue. On tape playback there were a number of messages, among them: *"Will talk to you with love." "I'm back with you." "We thought you'd come. We know that. That is the truth. This is the truth. This is the light!"*

During this time Becky, who was sitting six feet away, recorded different messages. The first thing she taped was *"My mother."*

Four days later we visited the Coptic tombs. There must have been several hundred aboveground tombs in various states of disrepair. All one could see looking over the rolling hills and valleys were tombs and desert sand. Again I was almost overwhelmed with emotion, but this was far different from what I had felt in the small tomb by the pyramids. It was a feeling of peace and serenity, of wellness and joy. Each person in the group went his or her own way, and as I wandered alone, stopping at a tomb here and there, I would step inside the different ones that seemed almost to call out to me. At one place a clear female voice declared on the tape, *"I buried you,"* and later, *"This is my home."*

A never-to-be-forgotten experience was when eight of us sat in front of the Sphinx in Giza one night from ten P.M. until three A.M. The moon was full, and in the distance you could hear the chant of the muezzin calling the faithful to prayer. From time to time a member of the group would go and stand quietly in front of the Sphinx. Just before leaving I placed my portable tape recorder between its two paws and asked if anyone was present who had been there when the Sphinx was built. *"Very true"* was the soft but clear reply.

A month before we came to Egypt a small explosion had taken place in the Great Pyramid of Cheops. On national TV we were told the Egyptian government did not take the incident seriously, but the truth of the matter was different. Although visitors were still permitted in the King's Chamber, they had to enter it empty-handed. The gate to the Queen's Chamber was kept locked, and no one was allowed to enter. Fortunately I was able to make special arrangements to be admitted to the Queen's Chamber the day before we were to return home. Early that Saturday morning I entered the Queen's Chamber alone. My companion locked the gate behind me, promising to return in an hour. Many high-quality messages were recorded during that time, such as *"We come in. We stand here." "Come, that is friend."* Perhaps it is appropriate that the last two messages I recorded in Egypt were *"We come to you. Stay with you. We love you,"* and *"Sarah! We come to her."*

In April 1986 I returned to Egypt for seventeen days to teach an EVP workshop on location. Lynn Gardner, the leader of the 1984 tour, and I co-hosted the Egyptian Odyssey group in 1986. We had received warnings that we should cancel our trip because of terrorist activity. Lynn and I did not take the warnings lightly and discussed the pros and cons of such a trip at that particular time. Our feeling was "Go!" but we consulted with members of the group before making a final decision. It was unanimous— we would go.

Security was tighter than two years before, especially at the airports, but we never felt threatened. The Egyptian people were as warm and friendly as on the first trip. Several members of our group said at the end, "The best thing about this experience was meeting and getting to know the Egyptians."

Voices of the invisibles continued to speak to me through my tape recorder. At locations visited two years earlier I said, "I have come back to you." Several messages recorded at such times seemed to be follow-up messages from the first trip. A few voices sounded the same as in 1984.

At the small tomb that had moved me so deeply earlier, I asked the unseen to bring back the person who had said *"My mother"* the first time. A loud, shrill Class A voice replied, *"He's coming back! We encourage him."*

The open sarcophagus at Memphis and the room used for magic rites at Dendera, where I had received pleas for help, were revisited. Lynn and I held private sessions at both and gave suggestions to help the entities move on. At Dendera especially, I had the impression we were being listened to very carefully by a number of the invisibles. A sense of calmness seemed to grow and eventually prevail in the small crypt.

Two areas visited for the first time in 1986 were Saint Simeon's Monastery, located near Aswân, and the church of Zeitoun, in Cairo. Standing in Saint Simeon's cell, which dates back to A.D. 500, I asked for a message. A clear, deep male voice, perhaps demonstrating a quality Saint Simeon needed in his earth-plane life as leader of his monastery, said, *"I come with patience."*

At the church of Zeitoun, famous for the apparition of the Virgin Mary that appeared a number of times to thousands in 1968, I taped two messages while sitting quietly in the sanctuary. The last message recorded was also the last message taped in Egypt on that trip. A clear voice said, *"I love you."*

Egypt. Land of history. Land of mystery. Few people can visit there and remain untouched. It continues to call to what is buried deeply within.

Chapter 13—The Voices and Other Worlds

> Our normal waking consciousness, rational consciousness, as we call it, is but one special type of consciousness, whilst all about it, parted by the filmiest of screens, there lie potential forms of consciousness entirely different. . . .
>
> —William James

Other worlds. It is enough to tell people you talk to the dead. Once you mention worlds and realities not commonly thought of as spirit, and go on to hint that you feel you are sometimes in contact with them, you are liable to find that even those who accepted the possibility of this type of communication are no longer so accepting. Yet spirit contact is only part of the story.

For over three years I believed all my contacts came from the dead. That was enough. Despite my skeptical and at times pragmatic inclinations, I had found it necessary to undergo major changes in my beliefs as I crossed the bridge to the dead and as they crossed the bridge to me. Still, having what I hope is a healthy degree of skepticism, while realizing the need to be practical, I have learned that if we wish to develop our consciousness to the fullest, we must eliminate false boundaries. If we can remain open to the possibility that what we think we know about reality is only partly true, or even false, and our horizon, which is self-imposed, is nothing more than the limit of our individual, personal sight, we may then begin to venture into new lands that appear infinite. The journey is not for the fainthearted. We can easily become lost and flounder about in confusion. If we would travel to unknown and unseen worlds, we must place trust in our contacts from beyond to protect us. One of the first lessons we learn as we begin our journey into unknown realities is that the more we learn, the more we realize how much we don't know. Since there are no limits to what lies beyond, it stands to reason that our journey will, if we choose, never end. The best we can hope for is to expand our consciousness to catch a glimpse of where we, and others, are now in development and realize that each person has the potential to take part in the ongoing process of creation.

Early explorers, such as Columbus and de Soto, may only have had a hazy idea where they were going and where they hoped their travels would end. In spite of the dangers and uncertainties that surrounded their adventures, they had an important advantage: they knew that eventually their trip must end because they were operating within the finite limits of earth.

Those of us who venture outward, who make contact with other worlds, other dimensions, other realities, have no such assurance. It is frustrating, once a link is formed with another dimension, not to know what dimension it is. You ask them to tell you the name of their world, from what reality they come. Occasionally an answer may be received, but usually not. It could be that their world does not have a name, that they have found names, labels, unnecessary. Names, in themselves, have no meaning. They are only a tool, a convenience, to help us carry on our earth-plane life. This does not make one reality, or world, better than another. It helps, though, to give us a glimpse of what reality may be like for another dimension.

In the reading I had done, before and after starting to work with tape-recorded voices, I had read a few of what might be called metaphysical books. Some I found so unbelievable, I put them aside after fifty pages or so. Others stirred my interest and gave me something to think about. Are there UFOs? Do they come from points out in space, known and unknown to us? Are we surrounded by other realities, where active conscious life is being carried on, life probably different from our own but as fulfilling to its inhabitants as our reality is to us?

Once I had established lines of communication with the spirit world I decided to ask them questions about these issues. Realizing they might not know a great deal more than I did, I nevertheless hoped that from their unique position they would have some factual answers to my questions.

One of the first questions I asked the spirit voices was whether there are realities in addition to the earth plane and spirit-world realities where entities exist who have consciousness and a sense of *"I."* Someone answered, *"That's true."*

This could be considered a leading question—which I try to avoid as much as possible; however, sometimes, in order to start a new avenue of exploration with the other side, it is necessary to ask this sort of question. When I do ask such questions, I then seek additional confirmation by rephrasing my later inquiries.

Twenty-four hours after the *"That's true"* message I repeated my question along with their response. I asked if I had interpreted their reply correctly. This time a voice said, *"Did,"* and two counters later added, *"I share now with you."*

The possibility of there being a parallel universe is another hotly debated subject. The spirit world could be called a parallel universe. My question as to there being such a world was answered by two different voices, both Class A. The first, speaking in fast tempo, affirmed, *"Yours is the biggest."* One counter later, the second individual added, *"Yes, it's there."*

In the next recording I asked if I had recorded their two messages correctly. A clear female voice replied, *"You certainly did,"* and three counters later added, *"You did hear it."*

The idea that any parallel universe would be exactly like our own, except in reverse, seems to be contradicted by, *"Yours is the biggest."* I suspect our conception of a parallel universe may be mistaken. Perhaps we should eliminate the word "parallel." One dictionary definition of the word is "precisely corresponding." From what has come through my tape recorder, there seem to be many universes coexisting alongside our own universe, but evidence so far suggests that what constitutes life for us may not for them. That we don't see them, and for the most part are unaware of them, does not mean they aren't there.

This is similar to a situation sometimes created by a stage hypnotist. He will summon several volunteers from the audience to the stage and hypnotize them; yet before snapping them out of trance he will contrive various antics. He may command one woman on stage, for instance, to go around after she wakes up and shake hands with everyone on the stage. She won't shake hands with her husband, though, who is sitting beside her, also hypnotized, for she won't see him. The posthypnotic suggestion is then carried out, with the woman unable to "see" her husband three feet away.

Another area I tried to explore with the spirits in my early days of tape recording voices was that of UFOs. Here again, I didn't know if the spirits would know any more about them than I did, but their answers might be interesting.

Controversy persists not only about whether UFOs exist at all, but about what world, or worlds they come from if they do. Are these worlds within or without our own solar system, or are they psychic manifestations from alternate realities?

When I asked my spirit contacts if UFOs come from within our solar system, a loud, hoarse voice of unusual quality replied, *"Entirely."* The following day I asked why UFOs come to planet Earth and *"They did. A little bit of friendship"* was returned. Four counters later someone added, *"They said 'We have to fall, fall, through.' "*

Two months later I returned to the subject of UFOs and again asked if they came from other worlds and realities, receiving, *"That's right. Inseparable"* in response. Although this might be considered a leading question, too, the reply went beyond a simple yes or no. Someone tactfully reminded me my question was redundant. If UFOs come from other worlds, it stands to reason that the worlds they are from have different realities—in other words, the two are *"inseparable."*

Those on the other side at times use words to describe something of which we have no knowledge. When I asked if the beings of worlds UFOs come from survive death, a loud, clear voice gave the puzzling answer, *"They survive sheik."*

And so it continued. Every day I talked to spirits, and most days they replied. It did not occur to me to try to talk to anyone else. If it had, I would have discarded the idea as preposterous. There has been evidence for hundreds of years that the dead are able at times to make their presence physically known. I finally knew that one of these ways was by speaking through a tape recorder. From the reading I had done I could accept, barely, that there might be other worlds and realities besides the spirit world where conscious beings existed. They would not, I was sure, try to speak to me through my tape recorder. In the first place I didn't know if they used speech. I had in mind that beings from other realities were so much more evolved than we on the earth plane that their communication was mental. If, by chance, they did verbalize, they certainly would not have any interest in speaking to someone on tape. Additionally, taking this assumption to its logical conclusion, I felt I wouldn't be able to understand them even if they did. So I went blithely on. I was happy talking to spirits and hoped they were happy talking to me.

Every so often I was pulled up short by a message or a group of messages that did not sound as if they were coming from my spirit contacts.

One morning I recorded, *"Space will talk tonight."*

It is my policy to encourage everyone who attempts to speak to me. As I mentioned earlier, I always use words in my reply that my unseen communicants have used. If someone in the spirit world wanted to call him- or herself "space," it was fine with me.

In the second recording I referred back to the astral message and asked if space really wanted to speak to me that night. Immediately I was assured in a clear, partly singing voice, *"We'd like you to know that we'll be back to greet you."*

Not many could resist such an invitation, so that evening found me back at my tape recorder. I first called on the individual who had given the "space" message and asked him to tell me where he was.

"We have all come down" was the reply. Not knowing this had been received, I went on to ask whether they were inside my office. At once three messages, one after the other, were received from three different individuals.

"Yes."

"Near the books."

"Listen, Estep, I came down here."

Still having no idea I had anyone with me, I turned the microphone over to any "space" friends who wished to speak. A female voice said, *"I love you."*

When I played the tape back through the amplifier, I was astounded. To start with, all the messages were clear Class A and have since been duplicated and played for many people.

Analyzing the messages carefully, I saw that my visitors carried over from the morning the correct "person" in speech. *"We'd like you to know that we'll be back to greet you,"* I received in the morning; at night: *"We have all come down."*

The books they mentioned were the books on my office bookshelves located four feet from the tape recorder and me. They had to be in my office to see them. The voices were not typical spirit voices. The first two were almost "hard." All were very precise. Each voice had its own distinctive quality, and the female voice of *"Listen, Estep . . ."* was breathy. The entities sounded as if they were right where they said they were—in the office by my books.

During the recording, which lasted about five minutes, my dog, Misty, who was in the next room, was agitated. When I start to record, I usually close the door to my office, as I had done that evening. Occasionally Misty has been with me when I play a tape back and has appeared uninterested in the spirit voice phenomenon. That evening she growled and barked while I was recording—all of which is on the tape along with the paranormal voices.

It is interesting that they not only made an appointment with me in the morning to come back that night but they were in a position to know they would be able to carry it out.

Where did the voices come from? Were they of the spirit world or were they, as they claimed, from space? I didn't know.

The following morning when I asked how they came from their reality to mine a Class A voice answered, *"We find us a cord."* I tried to explore with them what the cord was, and they went on to explain it was a *"line."* Someone told me when I would put my line out, they would come. I am not at all sure what this means except that perhaps when I think of them, they pick it up telepathically.

Upon mention of space contacts, many people envision UFOs swooping helter-skelter through our skies. Those who claim to have seen beings from outer space give all sorts of descriptions as to their appearance. Alas, I can give none. They were invisible to me.

I wondered what I should do about the episode. Being cautious, and unable to arrive at any conclusion about this incident, however interesting, I did nothing.

One evening almost six months later, sitting down as usual with my tape recorder, I received three messages in less than a minute.

"Pro prosirus appearance is a, is a fact."
"This is an, an attack!"

"They headed up. They were practical."

All voices were clear, loud Class A. The first two messages were given in excited voices, and I was interested in the way several words were repeated. Also the words *"pro prosirus"* had no meaning to me, and I have spelled them phonetically.

Who were these entities who mentioned an attack? Although I have received a few messages in which I have been threatened and told I was hated, no one had ever mentioned any kind of a group attack, which seems to be indicated by, *"They headed up. . . . "* It was apparent someone was attacking someone else. The question also comes immediately to mind why these aliens, whoever they were, spoke English. The only explanation I can think of is that when I turn on my tape recorder, I put out some sort of "line," as they called it, and this "line" must automatically convert or program what they wish to communicate into language I can usually understand.

My attempts to find out more later that evening and the next morning met with silence.

Ten evenings later, when I again went to my tape recorder and asked if I had friends with me, I received the unexpected answer, *"They're cruising down."*

The next morning when I returned to the tape recorder and asked whether anyone was present, it seemed as if only a moment in time had passed for the other side. A female voice complained, *"It's so warm down here."*

During this same recording I asked if someone from their world had said, *"They're cruising down"* the previous evening. My question was not answered, but someone assured me, *"I'll fight for you."* Two counters after this a different voice added, *"Yes. You're very sweet."* My feeling is that these two entities were not talking to me but rather to each other.

A moment later I repeated my question as to whether one of them had given the *"cruising"* message.

With this they seemed to become aware I was trying to get through, for someone said, *"We're not with her,"* immediately followed by a different entity who told his companion, *"I am."*

I went on with my questioning and entreated them, if the cruising message had been theirs, to tell me where they were cruising. A loud voice answered, *"We're touring."* Not realizing that this or any of the previous messages had come through,

I asked why they were cruising. A voice that resembled Styhe's explained, *"We know them."*

After hearing these different messages, all of which had been Class A, I continued my inquiry in the second recording. I asked Styhe if he had been the one who'd stated, *"We know them."* Styhe confirmed, *"Yes, I am. It's a privilege to lead them."*

Here again I had a group of messages that did not fit the typical spirit communications pattern. I was further confused by Styhe's involvement with this unknown group. From the time he had first begun to speak to me, I had viewed Styhe as a member of the spirit world. He has answered many of my questions about the spirit world and brought me friends and loved ones to whom I wished to speak.

Could it be possible for an entity to belong to spirit as well as space worlds? Might some of those I was in communication with be both spirit and space entities? I had no idea. Since I was starting to feel disoriented and not at all sure I wanted to muddy the waters calling other worlds besides the spirit world through my tape recorder, I stuck to "safe" questions. My questions were clearly aimed at spirits in the spirit world. Those on the other side must have been aware of my feelings, for they were careful not to expose me to situations that would further confuse me.

For six weeks I attempted not to think about space communications and realms. Several hundred messages came through during this time, all of which I could safely assume had come from spirits in the spirit world. Although I tried, I could not forget the three groups of atypical messages, as well as some less dramatic but nevertheless puzzling communications received over the years. In the end I decided I was being less of a person by running away. I owed it to myself and to others to reach out in friendship to anyone in any world or reality who wished to come to me in friendship.

There were dangers, I knew. I had read "horror" stories of those who claimed to have had close encounters with space aliens. I did not know if the contacts I was having were with space beings who could come into my office invisibly almost at will, or who communicated from hovering UFOs. This could possibly be happening, but I also believed I might be in touch with other realities—realities mystics claim to visit in trance. I had been skeptical of these claims in the past, but at least I had remained open-minded. Now it seemed as if, in spite of previous disbelief, I might also be in communication with alternate realities via my tape recorder.

Venturing into the unknown evokes considerable fear. Wisely or not, I felt no anxiety for myself physically. My greatest concern was that I might become so disoriented and bewildered by these contacts, I would be lost in a morass of confusion. I had to trust my own ability to withdraw from the contacts if this seemed advisable, as well as to trust my friends in the next dimension who have repeatedly claimed to help and protect me. The only way to discover if this trust could withstand being put to the test was to go ahead and speak to other realities directly.

Chapter 14—
Communicating
with Other Worlds

During the first recording the morning of March 31 for the first time I invited space friends to join me. For the minute I waited to hear from anyone who wished to communicate, I received five messages:

> *"You better come down."*
> *"They're in front of you."*
> *"I will come."*
> *"We will try to help."*
> *"Jeffrey, stay."*

The first two messages were Class A. The third and fifth can be heard without headphones.

After the minute had elapsed, I asked whether I had space friends with me. A high, clear female voice of unusual quality immediately replied, *"We know about you."*

It appeared my first deliberate attempt to contact space had been successful! Jeffrey! Like Styhe, I had always thought Jeffrey belonged to the spirit world. I again wondered if a spirit-world entity could also belong to space.

The message, *"We know about you,"* was interesting. It was obvious that if I was in contact with other worlds besides the spirit world, these other worlds had to know about me. I hadn't expected them to come back with a message that so clearly pointed this out, however. With the use of *"we"* the entity might be making some distinction between her world and the world of spirits.

A few days after my initial effort to contact space I asked if I had space or spirit world with me. Someone replied, *"All come down here."* Two counters later a different voice added, *"Yes, we can."* During the same recording I appeared to have both groups with me. *"That's right,"* a clear voice said, and one counter later a different voice responded, *"We're here. We came down. We're with them."*

In the next recording, when I asked if the two groups could see each other, I was assured they could. Later in answer to my question as to how the spirit world viewed extraterrestrials, the interesting and perhaps significant answer *"They start with me"* was returned in a Class A voice.

During the ensuing weeks I continued to further develop my channels with space. At the same time the spirit world remained important to me. I would spend one or two days talking to my spirit friends and then one or two days calling on space. Messages frequently came through from both worlds. It was difficult at times to tell with which world I was communicating. Although I always made it a point at the start of each day's recording to say which world I wished to contact, the two worlds' messages seemed at times to freely intermingle. I was just as likely to hear from Styhe and Jeffrey when I called on space as when I called upon the spirit world. Betty, an unknown friend who has spoken to me many times from the spirit plane, would also speak from space.

I considered two possibilities: one, that those in the spirit world were so anxious to talk to me, they would come through whether I called on space or spirit; or two, that some individuals, such as Styhe, Jeffrey, and Betty, although spirits, had moved out or on to a world not commonly thought of as spirit but rather space.

When we mention space, we tend to think of Mars, Venus, Jupiter, and so on. These are physical places with mass that can be located with a telescope.

Other space worlds, unknown to us, may also exist. They may have mass, like the planets in our solar system, but they may not. Life there could be fully conscious but nonphysical.

Each individual, through his consciousness, creates his own world and reality. This creation may be valid, or it may be distorted, but for the person it is real. It is not necessary for consciousness to be encapsulated within a physical form. An out-of-body experience shows that consciousness, freed from the physical body, can for a short time continue in a life of its own.

In the succeeding months many messages came from the spirit and other worlds. Some were startling; I had difficulty believing everything I heard. Slowly I became aware that when I called upon space, not all the voices had the same timbre. The majority sounded like spirit-world voices, but some had a high, almost mechanical quality to them. At times they had the peculiar habit of repeating certain words within their sentences. Now and then they would use words not found in any dictionary. It was as if they had learned my language well, but here and there their grasp of it was flawed. Messages from space entities would also sometimes be longer than the usual spirit entity. A few messages were fifteen to twenty words and even longer. The content of some of these messages was different, too, from spirit messages. Even more interesting, the voices from space did not seem to need to go through a learning process in order to speak on tape. Unlike spirit voices, many space messages were initially loud and clear Class A.

Bill Weisensale of Barstow, California, an experimenter in the field of the electronic voice and former editor and publisher of *The Spirit Voice*, has examined a number of my tapes. He wrote in an issue of *The Spirit Voice*:

> I spent the better part of one day studying one of Sarah's tapes on my oscilloscope. A few of the voices, notably some of those claiming to be from "space," exhibit a certain technical characteristic (background dropout), which indicates the presence of a very weak but otherwise normal radio signal. This effect is not present in ordinary communication from the spirit world, but it is the kind of thing we would anticipate in communication with extra-terrestrials. . . .
>
> Several of these voices give the impression of being mechanical or artificial, which is created by computer-controlled voice synthesis rather than by human means. Now, a voice synthesizer is obviously not the kind of thing

we would anticipate finding in use by the spirit world, but it is exactly the sort of thing we could anticipate in extraterrestrial communication, especially if for one reason or another the race doing the communicating had vocal cords unsuitable for pronunciation of human words.

A few weeks ago I called upon space for the first time in a month. Someone answered my question as to whether I had space friends with me, but the voice was speaking so slowly, I was unable to interpret what was being said. It occurred to me to push the FAST FORWARD button and play it back at 7½ instead of the usual 3¾. Immediately a loud, clear, mechanical Class A voice said, *"This lady's here. She may give me other light."*

During the same recording several other messages came through that could only be understood when they were played back at 7½. Most of us have heard the tonal quality of robots: the voices that spoke that day could be considered a close duplicate. My thought is that whatever mechanical synthesizer they use to speak to me had gotten out of synchronization with my equipment that morning.

Four days later I asked why I had been unable to understand the extraterrestrial messages unless I played them back at fast speed. Although I did not mention the "light" message, a clear Class A voice replied at normal speed, *"I went there seeking light."* This seemed to complement the earlier message when someone said that I might give the seeker *"other light."*

On several occasions the space voices have mentioned their spaceship. One morning an artificial-sounding voice said to me, *"The robot wants the lights on."* The space voices mentioned a black box they brought down to help them in their communications with me. When I tried to find out where the box had been placed, they remained silent. They have spoken about this box too many times for me to think it is not here, but it is apparently of a makeup incomprehensible to the human mind. They repeatedly say they are with me in my office, that they love me and help me; they say they need my help. I assure them of my love and friendship and that I want to help. When I ask how I can help, I receive only silence. It has occurred to me that perhaps they want their story told.

I have become acquainted with the names of certain of my space communicants. Since these individuals have never spoken in connection with the spirit world the way Styhe and Jeffrey have, I believe they may come from a nuts-and-bolts space world with mass. My space friends who have communicated by name to me are Ras, Seran, Vrom, A, the faithful Jule Bobo, and Howard Wilson (with a name like that I think he should be in the same spirit-space category as Jeffrey, but he never replies to my questions about the spirit world). Since my maiden name was Wilson, I thought he might be a long-lost relative and greeted him fondly the first time he gave his name. In the family Bible, which traces the Wilson genealogy back several hundred years, there is no Howard to be found. He might somehow have been overlooked, but then, the name Wilson is such a common one, he may not be related.

Ron Stallings talks about a close encounter he had at the age of thirteen, when a spaceship landed near a lake where he was fishing and took him aboard for a physical examination. One evening he urged space to speak through his tape recorder. A number of loud, clear messages came from entities who said they were in a nearby spaceship. One of them introduced himself as *"Mr. Wilson."* This was several months before I heard from Howard. One must wonder if it could be the same Wilson.

Twelve days after I first spoke to space a clear voice said, *"You have sure friends here."* The following day I asked what sure friends I had had with me twenty-four hours earlier. Someone suggested, *"Look right beside you. They're four side, beside you."* I inquired whether these sure friends were from space. My question was answered with, *"Yes, I want to come back near you. I want to come down. I want you come back. Once you saw. Charlie go back."*

Those in space mention taking me on a tour of their world. As far as I know, unless it has happened in the dream state, I have traveled nowhere.

For the most part, although I see no physical manifestation of space or spirit entities while recording, I have caught occasional brief flashes of something. This is so ephemeral, disappearing almost as quickly as I see it, that it is hard to describe. Briefly, these "objects" are round, smaller than a dime but about the same color. I asked Styhe what they are, and he answered, *"They're life."* When I asked whether the objects have consciousness, he said, *"Some."*

Several times I have picked up the word *"Venus."* From our

space probes we have learned that biological life as we know it cannot exist on Venus. Any life possibly existing there must be different from anything we know, and as I suggested earlier, life on such a world could be one of pure consciousness.

I tried to further explore the idea that a spirit may live a conscious, if not biological, life in another world before reincarnating back to the earth plane. My question as to whether some of us have done this was answered with, *"There's one in twenty."*

During the first recording one morning a loud, clear Class A voice proclaimed, *"A Martian here."* Three counters later he added, *"I'm board ship."* In the next recording I asked him to tell me where his spaceship was. The voice, still Class A, replied, *"We got here with you."*

On several occasions I have also been told my communicators came from Alpha Centauri. In March, when I asked if a certain voice of unusual quality had come from space, a clear male voice replied on the reverse side of the tape, *"Alpha Centauri know, know that we can."* Fifteen counters later he added, *"Alpha Centauri is my house."* (I should stress that I had never mentioned Alpha Centauri to anyone through my tape recorder before taping these two messages.) Three months later, again completely unsolicited, and still on the reverse side of the tape, a voice informed me, *"Alpha Centauri is here to give my power."*

We are told by space scientists that there is no life on Mars or Alpha Centauri. I certainly would not try to argue otherwise, but when a being emerges who tells me he is aboard a space ship or that he is from Alpha Centauri, I have to wonder about the scientists' conclusions.

One Sunday I was feeling discouraged as I sat down to record. I said nothing about how I was feeling, however, and, after the usual introduction, asked if there was a ship from space close to my home. Immediately two different voices, both Class A, replied. The first voice told me, *"We bring spaceship,"* followed by the second individual who added, *"We could give her encouragement."*

I was greeted one morning upon inviting my space-world friends to join me by an extremely loud, clear voice with *"Hi! Deena!"* This is interesting and important. Other experimenters working independently in the field of electronic voice have recorded the name Deena. One of the messages that Dan McKee of Illinois has recorded is *"Deena."* When the "Deena" voices on our two separate tapes are compared, they sound similar. Another friend recorded *"Deena"* several years ago, and it is her feeling it came from space.

The conclusion that because each of us has received this word, there must be such a person or place somewhere, is difficult to escape.

Once when I expressed my sorrow over not being able to see the entities I communicate with, someone said, *"Lift your eye."* I lifted it but still saw nothing. Since then I look up frequently. My contacts must be aware of what I am doing, because not long ago someone uttered, *"Your eyes look up."* This was followed with, *"Love that girl"* and finished by, *"That's Sarah."*

During an afternoon recording six months ago I asked if I had friends from space with me. A voice answered, *"We're next behind you."*

In the second recording I countered that I had looked but hadn't seen them. Why was it, I asked, they could see me, but I couldn't see them? Usually such a question has brought no answer, but this time was different.

"We stay, stay in the matter," a voice replied. This was followed with a loud male voice that added, *"Want to leave it."*

The next day when I asked them to confirm the statement that they stayed in the matter, a clear Class A voice said, *"We stay in your office."*

If it is true that they *"stay in the matter,"* this would help to explain why I, and others, do not usually see space entities. What part of the entity is in (the) matter? To me, it seems as if it must be their consciousness and that those who communicate with us, or who approach us up close, do so in an out-of-body state.

The message, *"Want to leave it,"* is also interesting. It suggests that the individual is not satisfied with the status quo and that perhaps he wants to materialize for us. Some entities seem able to achieve this to a certain degree. The small objects I catch glimpses of may be a partial or full materialization.

More recently, when I repeated my question as to why I can't see them, someone answered significantly, *"You can in your concept."* He indicated by this message that I see them in my own way, but this is not the way they actually are. We in this reality have been conditioned to see only certain things. How much, I wonder, happens around us merely a "touch" away, of which we remain unaware?

One time a clear voice declared, *"We have listening craft."* When I asked in a later recording why their listening craft came to planet Earth, an uneven, mechanical-sounding voice responded, *"To help man. That is something to by now there."* Not all of this computes, but this is not unusual sometimes when I communicate with worlds other than spirit. The marvel is that they get through as well as they do.

My home is located on a tributary of the Chesapeake Bay. We have a large porch in front of the house that overlooks a yard sloping down to the water two hundred feet away. In warm weather we like to sit on the porch and watch the boats going by. I had never mentioned this porch to the other side.

Shortly after I began communicating with space, the extraterrestrials started referring to the porch and told me they would be there at night and wanted me to go there also.

Just two days after my first effort to contact space, someone said, *"The one sit porch if he came."*

Eight days later, on a warm spring evening, I told the space beings I was going out to the porch and would be happy to see them there if they wanted to come down. A clear voice replied, *"I'll find her there if somebody will help us."* Although I went out to the porch carrying my battery-operated tape recorder in the hope I might receive voices on tape, nothing could be heard on playback but the traffic passing on the highway two miles away. I saw nothing paranormal.

Nine days after this I again said I would go to the porch and invited them to come down and be with me. This time someone assured me, *"We'll be right there down to see you."* When I asked if these individuals were from space, a loud voice of unusual quality exulted: *"I found the link."*

One morning a voice said, *"We'll call her."* This was immediately followed with, *"Come out tonight."*

In the next recording I expressed willingness to meet them on my porch. A voice replied, *"I'll help this evening."*

That evening I spent an hour on the porch but saw nothing, and there were no paranormal voices on tape.

The next morning I told my contacts I had been on the porch and wondered if anyone had been there with me.

A clear voice answered, *"We led down three."*

Not knowing this had been received, I repeated my question. A voice answered, *"When they come back, they zoom."* This was followed by a different voice telling me, *"They come down when you're in faithful."*

All of this is interesting. They made an appointment with me in the morning for that evening. I kept the appointment, and so did they. The message, *"We led down three,"* makes one wonder in what manner the three entities were *"led down."* Many times I have received word that these beings not only help me, but there also seems to be a group of guides among them who help other entities who want to communicate. This was apparently such a situation. The word *"zoom"* brings all sorts of mental images of entities zooming back to "something" when they leave me. Notice the unusual structure of the final sentence *"They come down when you're in faithful."* I am sure they meant that when I am faithful in trying to contact them, they come down. Despite dissimilarities in our worlds, the space beings exhibit some human characteristics. We treasure one who is faithful to us and try to repay in kind.

One day I asked whether they had a sense of time in their world. A voice replied, *"Our theory is we came here; it is the same."* I believe I was being told that when my space contacts enter my world, time for them will be the same as for us.

It occurred to me that if they have the ability to speak on tape, perhaps they might be able to come through on my television screen. After a series of questions lasting several days to gauge their willingness to appear on TV and their accord, I asked where I should tune my set. They directed, *"Thank you. Will repeat. At night forty-seven."*

From their message I had to infer they had told me before to turn to 47, but I hadn't been aware of it.

That night I sat in front of my television viewing 47 UHF, awaiting the show. All I saw were millions of black-and-white dots, commonly known as "snow," in front of my eyes. After ten minutes of this, I reached a near hypnotic state and decided I'd seen enough.

Three nights later, to my shock, I saw U S C A roll across my screen in capital letters one after another. They started near the top on the left side of the screen and rolled across it to the right. Each letter was visible for approximately two seconds before disappearing into the next. They seemed to be composed of the "snow" on the screen and yet were somewhat darker and superimposed on the dots.

Although I have never been hypnotized, I decided that looking at the screen in this way must induce self-hypnosis. It was just my imagination, I thought.

The next morning at my tape recorder I mentioned the letters I had seemed to see the evening before. Several messages were returned, indicating the letters had actually been there.

Twenty-four hours after U S C A rolled across my screen, the letters V E N U S appeared in the same way. Finally I had a word that made sense . . . or did it? Occasionally I had taped *"Venus"* through my recorder; now I saw the word on my television screen.

The next day I again tried to confirm my viewing of the night before. I avoided mention of the word "Venus" but asked if they had shown me the name of their world. Several answers ensued: *"We did. We talk to you." "We will operate. We will come." "We're by with A."*

Six nights later A R R I V E D rolled across my screen.

Twelve hours after this, when I asked about the word, I taped, *"Yes. We can talk with you."* It is interesting that the message was basically the same as that received six mornings earlier, *"We talk to you."*

I was not able to go every night to my television, and many nights when I did, nothing was visible. Until now all that had come through were capital letters, a development I certainly hadn't expected.

Thirteen nights after A R R I V E D was seen, the first picture came through along with words. There was a round disk with four or five slash marks from two to seven o'clock. To the left of the second and third slash marks, was a black dot. Under the picture was the word V E N U S.

The impact of the picture and word aside, it is interesting that for the second time V E N U S had appeared on my screen, and even beneath the picture the space beings had continued to spell it with capital letters.

Six nights later a picture of a man emerged, shown from the shoulders up. His eyes were closed; he had long hair. Five minutes later, on the lower right-hand corner of the screen, there was a side view of a man running off the screen—right to left.

When I asked on tape the following morning if they had sent a picture of themselves, or an associate, through my television the night before, I was told, *"Yes, we did."*

For the next six weeks I went occasionally to my television. At times I may have seen something, though I couldn't be sure. Watching an inactive channel for any length of time is extremely hard on the eyes. My TV watching had to be confined to late at night, when I was tired, and I usually ended up falling asleep in front of the screen.

Finally something came through that I couldn't dismiss: A series of dominoes tumbled quickly across the center of the screen. They looked like typical dominoes and remained in view about three seconds.

The next morning I mentioned the dominoes during the recording. *"You have twenty"* was taped. Later, when I again asked for confirmation that they had sent the dominoes through my screen, someone said, *"Yes, we did."*

Two days later came the most startling picture of all received during the several months I sat in front of my television. A group of five to six figures, seemingly male, ran as if in formation. They first appeared slightly to the right in the center of my screen. The run was controlled, and they moved from the right to the left of the screen. A three-dimensional side view was shown. Each figure was dressed identically in what looked like a silver-gray uniform. Each figure's head was fully covered from crown to shoulders in a loose hood, which was the same color as the uniform. The figures were of normal size and seemed to be the same height. They were in view about four seconds, and during this time the "snow" disappeared from the screen.

Later my questions about these figures and why they had been running brought a puzzling Class A response. A male voice replied, *"They were presentenced here."*

During this viewing, as well as one or two earlier ones, my dog, Misty, paced around the TV room, growling, hair bristling, showing great agitation. Finally she came and sat against my leg, quivering and whining—behavior very atypical for her. My words of comfort had little effect. When I later commented about this on tape, calling Misty "my dog," a clear voice replied, *"Your pet knows when we're around it."* I found it interesting that instead of "parroting" back my word "dog" they used the word "pet," thereby showing that they knew what Misty was to me.

Since then I have sporadically sat in front of my television. At times I have seen additional capital letters, not signifying a great deal to me, as well as one or two pictures of individuals.

Recently I bought a VHS video recorder. In time I hope to establish contacts with other worlds through my TV and have a record on tape of what may come through on the screen.

In December, when ice first formed on the river for the year, a space entity asked, *"Is that thick water?"* It is difficult to escape the conclusion that the questioner, who was speaking to someone else, came from a world in which ice is unknown. From this simple query, we can form a tentative idea of the climate of his world. Even though we still don't know the name of his home, we can at least eliminate a few planets on which we know ice is found.

One morning when I asked if they have seasons in their world, someone replied, *"We look like yellow."*

In the second recording I asked if the predominant color in their world was yellow, as we call planet Earth green? At once someone let me know I was incorrect by replying, *"Say! I say, say not!"* I again repeated my question about seasons in their world and was answered with, *"That's right."*

The following morning a loud Class A voice I have heard many times before said, *"We'll sit, sit by the window."*

Thirty-six hours later, at about 8:30 P.M., I was in my office reading, where I sit every evening. My chair faces the window, and something caused me to look up. I saw a round yellow sphere, the size of a basketball and about the color of the moon, slowly floating down outside my office window. It was in view approximately three seconds before vanishing in front of my eyes.

I was happy to see this physical manifestation from my friends but, strangely enough, not surprised. To me it was further evidence of the validity of our contact with one another. I could also better understand their messages of the last several days:

"We look like yellow" was their telling me what color they would be when I saw them.

"We'll sit, sit by the window" informed me where they would be when the manifestation took place.

The entire episode provides much food for thought.

Here again the extraterrestrials demonstrated their ability to plan ahead and to follow through with their plans. Close to sixty hours had passed from *"We look like yellow"* until the time I saw them. They showed by the manifestation that they know where I spend my evenings.

Interesting as all this is, it presents us with more important questions.

Did I see a physical manifestation of an intelligence from some world known or unknown to us? Or had this merely been an object guided down by entities for me to see but without innate intelligence of its own? Finally, could one or more intelligences have been riding in the sphere, using it as a vehicle to come from their world, or reality, to our own? Remember the two messages *"We look like yellow"* and *"We'll sit, sit by the window"*: Whether the yellow sphere was them, or something in which they were traveling, I don't know, but I believe they were there.

My questions the next day about what I had seen the previous evening confirmed that the sphere had indeed been from space. When I turned the microphone over to space friends for a message, a clear voice said, *"We see there. We can see after her. Yes, look after her."*

I developed a physical problem a few days after this brief encounter. It began as a strange outbreak on my arms, which then spread to my chest. At first it looked like a rash, but here and there unsightly sores erupted. Although it was July, I wore long-sleeve shirts, which I kept buttoned up to my neck so no one could see. Naturally I wondered if this was related to the object I had seen outside my office window. I should mention that never before or since have I had any sort of skin condition. After two weeks and no sign the rash was healing, the irritation drove me to a physician. He was puzzled and said he'd never seen anything like it. To him it looked more like shingles than anything else, but because I was not experiencing any pain, he couldn't identify it. Call it a lack of courage, if you will, but I refrained from mentioning what had happened two weeks earlier. He prescribed several medicines, and within a week the condition was gone.

There is one memento of the encounter that lasts even today. A fresh red rose was sitting on the windowsill perhaps three feet away from the sphere when it came down. Ten days later it was just as fresh as the day I placed it there. Normally, cut roses, in the summer, wither and need to be thrown away after several days. I began watching it, not changing the water or touching it, and after two weeks it took on a dried-up appearance. It remains on my windowsill, having lost little of its color, but looking almost the same as it did when I first put it there several years ago.

During the second recording one morning a Class A voice said, *"My God is with you."* In the next recording I asked the name of their God, and a monotone voice answered, *"We have different God. Someone knows everywhere. Something knows that a group will come down."* Here is another example of a message that does not entirely compute, but the meaning may still be clear. They imply that, as we do, they perceive their God as omniscient. When I asked if they had more than one god, someone replied, *"Yes, there's lots of them."*

I have tried to show we are surrounded by known worlds that may be communicating with us. In addition, there are many other realities existing that, although aware of us and capable of interacting with us, remain outside human knowledge.

I am heartened by those who speak from other worlds—they express love and friendship and a desire to help, emotions that are familiar to me. Most of those who communicate through my tape recorder I have not known, but I have never felt they were strange creatures. There is a kinship, a bond, between all forms of life, whatever shape or consciousness they take, wherever their world is found. If we in this dimension, in this world, reach out to other realms in friendship and in honesty, we can share qualities that we, as humans, value. What does it matter if other beings are nonphysical, or if their physicality is beyond our imagining? They have shown that in what is essential—love, respect, and a reverence for life—we are the same.

Chapter 15—The Work of Other Experimenters with Electronic Voice Phenomena

It seems that EVP researchers are going to have to prove [the existence of EVP] beyond the shadow of a doubt before the scientific community will have anything to do with it. So it's a rather lonely road we're going down and we have one another for needed verification and encouragement and to keep going when the progress seems slow and discouraging.—Dan McKee, Illinois State Coordinator for the American Association–Electronic Voice Phenomena (AA–EVP)

The voices will speak to John and Jane Doe. If they spoke only occasionally to a few select people their genuineness might be in doubt, but this is not the case. They do not limit themselves to a handful of experimenters who, like Merlin, could conjure something out of nothing. They are worldwide. They speak on tape for hundreds, and the number grows as others, learning about them, sit down in front of a tape recorder and ask "Is anyone here?"

Some experimenters are noted for their outstanding success in taping voices. What distinguishes a Friedrich Jürgenson of Sweden from John Doe of Middletown, U.S.A., though, is not entirely clear. Time and effort spent are certainly important factors, but the psychological, philosophical, and spiritual attunement with those in the next dimension, I would venture to say, is even more important.

England has Raymond Cass and Gilbert Bonner; Germany, Edelgard John, Luise Fuchs, Bernadette Arras, Hans Otto Konig, and Dr. Ernst Senkowski. In Italy we find Virginia Ursi, Marcello Bacci, and Capitani. Bacci and Capitani use an old World War II shortwave set with tubes. They turn it on and engage in clear two-way conversations with the unseen. Frequently the voices speaking are so loud and clear that everyone in the room can hear and interpret what is being said and can reply or ask additional questions. The unseen group communicating with them is unique because at the end of each session they begin singing. The singing, which may last for a minute, has been studied by musicologists. No one has been able to interpret any of the words. It is as if a heavenly chorus has just burst into song, and the sound is indescribably beautiful.

It is not amiss to take a look at some other experimenters who have succeeded in making firm contacts with the next dimension.

Raymond Cass of Yorkshire, England, although he seldom tapes now, was at one time a leading European experimenter. In an interesting letter to me he described his own work as well as Raudive's and Jürgenson's discoveries in the field. He wrote about the very faint voices often received and how many experimenters try to "extract humanoid voices out of the pervasive white noise of the microphone or diode."

He goes on to say:

"Friedrich Jürgenson described quite another phenomenon. He was at the receiving end of a series of strong transmissions from an extrinsic and unknown source. Jürgenson stabilized the contacts to the point of dialogue with the voice source.

"Strong audible voices of what Jürgenson called the central transmitting agency have been heard on all frequencies all over the world. If an investigator gets to be electronically tagged by this mysterious agency, he will receive from time to time strong extrinsic voices metamorphosing normal radio broadcasts, singing lustily, or perhaps making doom-laden and gloomy predictions.''

Regarding Konstantin Raudive Mr. Cass writes:

"He recorded thousands of faint, almost inaudible, whisper voices which by virtue of his linguistic skill he invested with meaning, meaning which, alas, careful investigators were unable to confirm. Nevertheless, he also recorded many authentic transmissions from the enigmatic source. He was not so self-deluded as many have thought. . . .

"Between Jürgenson and Raudive, these two pioneers have helped tear down the barrier between this existence and coexistent worlds. . . .''

In a separate letter to me Mr. Cass wrote that when he was taping he used a portable radio set on the air-band between 125 and 134 MHz for his sound source. He mentioned in this same letter that he felt it important to differentiate between loud and audible voices breaking onto radio frequencies and very faint, almost inaudible, whispers or monosyllables appearing on diode and microphone recordings. He feels there is a *generic* difference, two distinct species of voices, one from extrinsic transmitted sources and the other possibly using the energies of the experimenter.

Mr. Case believes, as Jürgenson does, that the strongest, clearest voices come from a central transmitting agency. This may sound extreme, but I have taped messages indicating there is such an agency.

Gilbert Bonner of Sussex, England, is another well-known EVP taper. He has been working for a number of years in the field and has published articles about it in various publications.

In a letter to me he wrote:

"Any tape recorder should be able to record paranormal voices within the limited frequency range at 100 to 3,000 Hz, but cheaper ones may not pick up as well or give full-range realism to speech obtained on a hi-fi machine covering say 40 Hz to 6,000 Hz.

"The method of recording from radio that I adopted

allows voices to be received whether transmitted by EM [electromagnetic] waves or 'metamorphosed' from existing radio material by some PK [psychokinetic] effect. Generally I tune to a frequency of the medium wave band that is near 1500 KHz. I allow radio stations to fade in and cut . . . a beating effect, provided they are foreign stations and not broadcasting in English. Care is needed to get the signal-to-noise ratio correct, or voices can easily be masked by the radio. I have also made good recordings on shortwave near 31 meters. . . . I prefer to work with the 'open microphone' method rather than direct patch cord. I often use stereo mikes, one in front of the speaker, and one for me to speak into. Recordings may appear on either track, and I have noted several times a strange thing. Voices coming in from one track may suddenly switch to the other track (or channel). Some sound source is essential, either as a carrier, as an energy source, or to provide the raw material from which voices are fabricated. One thing that is essential in voice research is PATIENCE.''

Mr. Bonner noted a difference in background sound when using a shortwave receiver as the sound source rather than a radio. He finds fewer radio intrusions but more atmospheric sound with shortwave. Mr. Bonner closed his letter by saying that one UK researcher, a physicist, is trying to investigate what effect gravitational fields may have on the voices.

Another taper in the British Isles who is having good results with her recordings is Tina Laurent of Wales. Tina learned about the voices in August 1983, just before she moved from the United States back home to Britain. She was so enthusiastic that she started taping, using a small battery-operated tape recorder, on the plane back to Wales. Voices came through, high in the sky, and she has continued with her work ever since. She has made steady progress with her voices, and now receives many that are solid Class A quality. Tina and her recordings are frequently mentioned in various Welsh publications, and she appears to be one of very few people in her country communicating with the unseen through a tape recorder.

Germany is the country with the largest number of people recording voices or having an interest in the phenomena. This interest dates back to 1968, when Konstantin Raudive published his research in the German book *The Inaudible Becomes Audible* (translated into English in 1971 under the title *Breakthrough*). In the 1970s the German VTF (Association for Voice Taping Research) was started by Hanna Buschbeck so that all those interested in the voices could exchange ideas and discoveries and meet together at national conferences. Today, with a membership of more than one thousand, the group is led by Dr. Fidelio Koberle of Düsseldorf, West Germany. Conferences are held yearly and a quarterly journal is published.

Several years ago Hans Otto Konig of West Germany began a similar group called the FGT (Research Association for Voice Taping). This group is involved in research and development of equipment and methods to improve the quality and length of communication with the unseen. Conferences are held every so often for members and other interested individuals.

Konig is studying the area of ultrasonics and working with light frequencies such as infrared and ultraviolet to try to enhance the quality of the voices. He has given many live demonstrations using his electronic system at conferences as well as on Radio Luxembourg. In January 1983, while being interviewed over the radio, he taped the message, *"Otto Konig makes wireless with the dead."* This was heard by hundreds tuned in to the program and created quite a stir. His messages come directly over the speakers and can be heard by every listener. The unusual clarity of his communications has impressed all who have heard them.

There are those in our own country who are trying to improve intercommunication with the invisibles through research and development of recording equipment.

In April 1982, George Meek, founder and president of MetaScience Foundation of North Carolina and an engineer with an international reputation for his many inventions and patents, startled the world when he announced at Washington's National Press Club that he and his associates had electronic proof that we survive death with the mind and personality intact. They had developed a system called SPIRICOM. The unusual and somewhat annoying sounds produced by SPIRICOM help the next dimension speak to us.

The tape George Meek played at the meeting was unlike anything heard heretofore in spirit communication. The main spirit communicator was scientist George Mueller, who died in 1967.

Dr. Mueller gave William O'Neil, one of Meek's associates, technical information about the system and how to improve reception. These suggestions, once implemented, worked, and mostly clear conversations, easily audible to anyone in the room, ensued over the speakers.

Eleven months before introducing SPIRICOM to the rest of the world, Mr. Meek contacted me and asked if I would agree to work with it in the hope that O'Neil's results could be replicated. I agreed, and a short time later SPIRICOM was brought to my home. The bulky, complex system was installed in my office, and I worked with it each morning and evening for a month. A number of voices, some Class A, were received during this time, but they could not be compared to the results of O'Neil.

Meek generously made available, at cost, all plans of SPIRICOM to the general public so those with technical know-how could build the system in the hope that a number of individuals could replicate O'Neil's results. Unfortunately no one who built it reported success. The general consensus is that O'Neil, who has strong and unique mediumistic gifts, combined those gifts with SPIRICOM, thus producing results.

We have other outstanding tapers in this country. In May 1982 I founded the American Association–Electronic Voice Phenomena (AA–EVP). As a result, I am fortunate in knowing most of the serious tapers in the United States. One of them is Dan McKee, who is the state coordinator of Illinois for the AA–EVP.

Dan is one of this country's most notable experimenters. He has been working in the field of EVP for twelve years, and the paranormal voices he tapes are unusually loud and clear. Dan seems to be tuned in to different realities, one of which is the spirit world.

In a letter to me he shared:

> I've used Dr. Raudive's methods and have had some success with the air-band system you use. I used an RF [radio frequency] signal generator to artificially create the carrier—in fact, two generators—but with limited success. In the course of working with the voices it became apparent to me that they came through best when given some kind of background noise or energy. Accidentally one night I ran a tape backward, and to my surprise,

heard words and sentences. I had as many as twelve consecutive sentences, which certainly refutes the claim of those who say they are recording random noises. The voices called me by my first name, my middle name, and my last name. Sometimes they answered my questions. Playing music backwards also works well. Occasionally they will mimic my voice, and they speak of my equipment and ways to improve reception.

Dan finds there are periods of high activity and periods of low activity but asserts, "There's a compelling desire that keeps me working and experimenting." He closed his letter by commenting that he had been associated with electronics one way or another for more than forty years. At one time he worked for the Federal Communications Intelligence Division, so "this background should make it difficult to fool me when it comes to the many possibilities that are offered as explanations for this phenomena."

David A. Lothamer, AA–EVP state coordinator of California, is another EVP taper who is gaining increasing recognition for his work with taped voices.

In a letter to me David made some general comments about recording paranormal voices. He noted, "It is my observation that NOISE, random or contrived, can be a variable in voice manifestation. In my own experiments I have utilized radio white noise, tape recordings of dripping water, music, and other noise sources. I use the *sound production–open-microphone method* almost exclusively.

"Virtually anything may be prerecorded and then used as a background noise source." David wrote that for the first several months he followed the advice of some experimenters to "sit in silence." He noted that the results he received were few and limited to whispers. Then he observed that "squeaks on the floor, the rustle of bedsprings, knocks on the door, seemed to spin off voicelike sounds that were above and beyond the accidental environmental noise." After David became convinced that sounds seemed to help the voices speak, he began deliberately using sounds as he recorded. From then on, the quality of his voices improved dramatically.

Ways to communicate with the unseen are continuing to evolve. In their book *Phone Calls from the Dead* D. Scott Rogo and Raymond Bayless report that the dead apparently try to communicate via telephone with friends and loved ones they have left behind. These calls, for the most part, were initiated by the other side. Now some experimenters in this country and others are deliberately calling on other dimensions using a telephone. They hook their phone up to a tape recorder so they will have a record on tape of any paranormal messages received.

Mercedes Shepanek, who before her death was the AA–EVP state coordinator of Virginia, worked in the EVP field for over eleven years. During this time she recorded thousands of excellent quality voices on both sides of her tapes. A year before her death she began trying to make contact through her telephone. In the Fall 1985 AA–EVP newsletter she reported:

> "I have been working with the telephone technique and have had some results, mostly whispers. Two of the transmissions were *"We will call you"* and *"We will ring you."*

> "This technique requires a telephone recording control (available from Radio Shack) and a telephone jack adapter. To convert your existing telephone jack to a "two-holer," you jack the device into the telephone wall jack along with your telephone and also into the mike and remote input of a cassette recorder. The method is as follows: Put the recorder into RECORD mode (it will not be activated until you lift the telephone receiver), lift the phone receiver, and dial any single digit. Make a brief announcement as you would in any tape session. You will have thirty-four seconds of clear line before the taped offer of assistance breaks in. Hang up and repeat the procedure. The obvious shortcoming is the brevity of the clear line time. An alternative is to arrange with a friend (preferably one acquainted with your strange life-style) to call at a preset time and leave his/her telephone off the hook for whatever period is agreed upon."

Clara Laughlin is the present AA–EVP state coordinator for Virginia. In the six years she has been taping she has established firm contacts with, apparently, more than one reality. Although most of her communicants are from the spirit world, now and then messages are taped from entities who claim they are space beings. Her main contact in spirit is an individual named Callie, a person she has never known, who tells her he is her "door-keeper." Callie brings to Clara those with whom she wishes to speak and also answers many of her questions, adding revealing comments of his own. Once after watching a Phil Donahue program about cryogenics, Clara asked Callie what the spirit world thought about this. Callie replied, *"A frozen soul gives no comfort."*

Carol Barron, state coordinator for Massachusetts, started taping at about the same time as Clara. She, too, has had many excellent, clear contacts with the spirit world. Carol finds that sounds are very important in helping voices speak. The spirits use almost any sounds she provides, and their voices tend to take on the quality of whatever sound source is heard in the background. Carol has investigated a number of supposedly haunted locations in New England and has frequently taped voices while out in the field. She has demonstrated electronic voice phenomena at colleges, making group recordings while doing so, and often with positive results.

Russian scientists are also involved in EVP research. Benson Herbert, an internationally known British parapsychologist, long skeptical that the voices were voices of the "dead," now feels they are most likely discarnate entities. This change of heart was brought about by the work of two Russians. In a letter to Tina Laurent, he quoted from articles written by these Russian scientists and said he guessed he'd have to become a spiritualist and an "EVPist."

In one article titled "Bio-Plasma and Psychic and Auto Regulation," Dr. Romen of the Alma-Ata University in the U.S.S.R. wrote:

> "Yoga and autosuggestion can deeply affect the bioenergetic processes in a person's system and is of great value in the prevention and curing of diseases and promoting regeneration . . . with the possibility of maintaining the personal 'I' (ego) on the conditions of extreme stress, and after death in a definite biological form. . . . This energetic image maintains the personal characteristics independently of spatial and temporal factors . . . and is a recognizable individual."

The other article quoted by Herbert was by Dr. G. P. Krokalev of Perm University, U.S.S.R., and is titled, "EVP" and says, "The human body can act as a receiver and a transmitter of radio waves. The skin acts as a transistor to modulate the waves so transmitting an audible sound via tissue and bones to the brain. . . . Concentration of thought can cause the ears to transmit faint sounds that can be picked up by a sensitive microphone and tape-recorded. . . ."

In his own EVP experiments Dr. Krokalev uses a plastic or rubber earcap, fitting around the ear, with a small hole in the middle for the insertion of a tiny microphone.

As briefly mentioned, we are continually discovering that contact with the dead need not be limited to voice contact through a tape recorder. Some people report messages coming from the beyond on their telephone answering systems. The invisibles are also affecting computers.

Ken Webster, an economics professor in England, started receiving messages five years ago through his home computer. The communicator claimed to be Thomas Harden, sixteenth-century dean of Brasenose College at Oxford. Enough information was provided by the dean for Webster to identify him positively as Harden. Webster has also received communication from a group claiming to exist in a parallel universe.

The voices are moving toward visual contact through our television sets. They have told some EVP researchers, such as Clara Laughlin, that they want to and will appear on TV screens. My own visual contacts were reported in Chapter 14. Before his death Klaus Schreiber of Aachen, West Germany, received instructions through his tape recorder as to how to set up equipment for television reception of pictures from the spirit world. He did this and felt he had taped pictures with his video tape recorder of his deceased daughter and mother.

It is encouraging that these beginning visual contacts are helping us move into more sophisticated methods of trying for a picture. A parallel is suggested between the early years of EVP recordings and the present state of TPP (television picture phenomena). The first voices were haphazardly recorded on tape, causing most people to think the tapes were faulty. When a few individuals realized this was not the case, they began deliberately to call on deceased loved ones. These efforts have grown to the current state of the art with continued research and development of better equipment and methods.

Unfortunately charges of fraud are made against EVP tapers today as have been made against other mediums from earliest times. This is especially true when results are outstanding. Whenever someone has unusually good contacts with the unseen, others try to duplicate these results by buying or setting up similar equipment. Each time, when a lack of success has ensued, accusations that the pioneer must be cheating have frequently followed. What the public fails to take into account is that equipment is only part of the story: It is the tapers themselves, with the unique energies and psychological makeup they bring to their recording sessions—qualities those in other dimensions can relate to—that are the most important factor in the phenomena. I have investigated situations where fraud has supposedly taken place and have never been convinced that such has actually been the case.

I am reminded of the time I watched James Randi, the magician who is skeptical of psi phenomena, demonstrate spoon bending on television. He feels everyone can bend spoons easily by cheating, which he quickly did for the television audience.

The same situation can exist for EVP; however, the reverse is also true. Just because we can demonstrate how voices can be produced fraudulently does not mean that they were.

Since I founded the American Association–Electronic Voice Phenomena in 1982, we have grown from the original number of twenty members to over two hundred who live in forty states, the District of Columbia, and twelve foreign countries. Ideas and discoveries are shared with all members through a quarterly newsletter. Enthusiasm is running high, and a number of members, as well as the general public, have attended the three national conferences held in the Baltimore area to date. Working together in our own international organization, sharing results freely with other groups around the world, and they with us, we are trying to break down the barriers that exist between this life and the next. In time we hope to remove the fear that has been a part of most lives since time immemorial—is there conscious life after death? Is there a sense of personal identity? More and more the evidence is piling up that these questions can be answered in the affirmative.

Chapter 16—A Visit to Luxembourg

Among those who work in the field of the electronic voice, most would agree that Jules and Maggie Harsch-Fischbach of Hesperange, Luxembourg, are the outstanding tapers in the world today. They began recording in 1984, but despite the relatively short time they have been communicating with other dimensions, the quality of the voices they have received, the uniqueness of the group that speaks, and the content of the messages that come through have impressed tapers everywhere.

When Maggie began recording, her husband, Jules, was a skeptic about the phenomena, but now the overwhelming evidence verified later through follow-up has caused him to accept that they are apparently hearing from more than one dimension. For the first year and a half their results were fairly typical of what other tapers receive. After that, though, Maggie was apparently "electronically tagged," and the communications steadily improved. They both work during the day but tape every night. The voices are so loud and clear as they come over the room speakers that they can be heard by everyone present. Two-way conversations, some very long, are thus possible. Many of the voices identify themselves, such as Konstantin Raudive and Henri Sainte-Claire Deville, a French physical and inorganic chemist who died in 1881.

The Fischbachs appear to be in communication with two main groups. There is the Life Stream group, composed of highly evolved personalities who had a life on the earth plane. They speak to the Fischbachs, via their tape recorder, with technical details handled by an entity who calls himself Technician. I have heard a number of tapes of the Fischbachs' communications, and Technician has a synthesized voice. It is above the level of a computer voice and yet is decidedly not human. Upon questioning, Technician has said that he never had an earth-plane life. To quote him: *"I am not human. I never incarnated. I am not and never was an animal. I am not energy, and I am not a light being. I was and still am a superhuman being and assigned to planet Earth."*

It is interesting the way Technician became a part of the Fischbach group. When I met the Fischbachs recently in Luxembourg, this was one of my first questions. Maggie explained that she had been in communication for some time with a young man on the other side whom we will call John. She asked John many questions about life after death, God, and the Bible, which John tried to answer. At the same time Jules was requesting technical assistance to help them in their tapings so they could receive louder and clearer voices. As Jules said: "I asked them to please send us a German technician, since I figured there were many more German technicians over there than from our own very small country of Luxembourg."

One day when Maggie asked John a question about God, a voice broke in and said, *"No. I will answer that question."* This marked the arrival of Technician, who has been a leading part of their group ever since. He brings many highly evolved personalities to communicate with the Fischbachs and their visitors from around the world who, upon hearing about the Fischbachs, have come to participate in a recording. Shortly after the advent of this guide, Maggie asked what they should call him, and he replied, *"You can call me Technician."*

In an early letter to me Maggie wrote: "He astounded us with his exceptional knowledge of electronics, physics, mathematics, astronomy, the natural sciences, and about the future and the past. . . . For us, he is the superhuman technician. He practices unconditional love, the kind that is unknown to us. In his words he says (they) recognize truth, everything positive, reverence and care for all life."

When Technician was asked what was necessary to establish taped communication with his world, he replied, *"An important prerequisite for contacts with our dimensions are a pure heart and a pure soul."*

During one session at the end of 1986 he said:

> *"The grief and suffering people bear and have to go through is a part of their inner self. Some of it is through their own action or initiated by higher forces in order to activate the learning process that leads to recognition, improvement, and perfection. . . . It is all closely connected and tied in with free will and choice of the individual, which God's power has granted to each of us as a great gift. . . . Without free will and choice there is no recognition of truth which comes from within. Therefore, blind obedience is not what higher powers want. . . . God prefers the seeker and those who question. No efforts are spared to advance human thinking and individual initiative from its low animal instincts to a position of spiritual thinking."*

The Fischbachs use, in accordance with technical advice from Technician, two communication systems. One is called GA 1. This is a two-way system that permits conversation back and forth between the observers in the Fischbach recording room, and those on the other side. It is similar to a telephone conversation and is normally just as clear. The GA 1 system can only be used when there are a limited number of people present.

The other system is named the Eurosignal-Bridge (ESB). It is used when there are many people in the room, and although the communications received are exceptionally clear and long, it does not allow two-way conversation. Technician has explained that each person gives off his or her own unique brain waves, and when there are more than four or five people taking part in a recording, it is more difficult for his side to come through. When this occurs, they must switch from GA 1 to Eurosignal as an electronic bridge from their dimension to ours.

Eurosignal is not something devised by the other side but is an actual personal calling system used in several countries of

Western Europe. It is similar to the system subscribed to by many professional people in our country who, when they hear a beep on their personal beeper, go to a nearby telephone and call their answering service or office. Although Eurosignal can be heard by everyone who tunes his radio to 88-90 MHz, in those countries who have the system, all he will hear is a series of electronic sounds that mean nothing to him. Those who subscribe to the system and pay a fee, are assigned a special code that their personal beeper picks up from the Eurosignal and lets them know that someone is waiting for them to call on the nearest telephone. Since it is a service that is paid for by its subscribers, the signal is heard twenty-four hours a day through the radio.

An example of a conversation held on the GA 1 system occurred in February 1987, between Dr. Ralf Determeyer, a West German researcher and engineer who was visiting the Fischbachs, and Technician.

> Dr. Determeyer: "Coming from such high levels of being, why do you speak to us in an Earth language such as German?"
>
> Technician: *"I have been addressed in your language. I could easily use other Earth languages."* (Speaks a Russian sentence.) *"You see, I could speak with you this way, too, if you could understand it."*
>
> Dr. Determeyer: "You could certainly readily explain the existence of the all-encompassing Spirit Being whom we call God."
>
> Technician: *"It would make no sense to explain God to you, for you cannot imagine God fully. Compared to a bucket full of water, your understanding is limited to a drop."*
>
> Dr. Determeyer: "Can transcommunication (EVP) contribute to world peace?"
>
> Technician: *"It is the most important instrument to awaken human consciousness out of early dawn's sleep. To do this takes bridges and bridge builders between your world and the world of spirit. You are a bridge builder."*

All of these answers, I would remind you, are clearly heard as they are given.

Recently the Fischbachs started receiving pictures through their television. Here again, directions for the complicated setup were given by Technician. Dr. Ernst Senkowski, a physicist and electrical engineer from Mainz, West Germany, and his wife, Adelheid, as well as several other individuals, were present during one television contact. Dr. Senkowski has been taping voices for years and is one of the most knowledgeable people in the transcommunication field in Europe. Some of the pictures received through the Fischbach television set showed landscapes and several people, one of them recognized as Hanna Buschbeck, founder of the German VTF, who died a few years ago. Technician explained that all pictures originated from the ''third level'' beyond death, where he says most of us go when we die.

The Fischbachs are also in communication with a group calling itself 2109. Jules and Maggie have started their own group interested in transcommunication—CETL (Cercle d'études sur la transcommunication Luxembourg). In connection with their group, they mail to all members a quarterly newsletter and have bought a home computer to help them run their organization. Three months after purchasing it unexplained messages started coming through the computer from the 2109 group, which says, like Ken Webster's group, that they are from a parallel world. Technician, incidentally, does not identify himself with 2109, although he knows about it. At one point when asked about them, he commented that if he were one of them he would *"be able to write on the computer, and that would be much simpler!"*

Maggie, Jules, and I have been corresponding for two years. They joined my association, the AA–EVP, in 1986, and from time to time would send me copies of their voice tapes. In one a member of the Life Stream group came through while visitors from Vienna were with them and gave a personal message for me. In it he said, *"We want to express by this way our satisfaction on the behavior of Mrs. Estep. Her position is quite all right. We approve."*

The Fischbachs and I hoped we could meet someday, and the opportunity presented itself at the end of October 1987. My husband and I flew to Luxembourg and were met by Jules and Maggie at the airport. The four of us immediately felt a close rapport, and as they drove us to our hotel in Hesperange, a short distance from their apartment, we chatted like old friends.

During the three days we spent in Luxembourg I learned many things about the Fischbachs unknown to me previously. My respect for them as individuals, and for the tremendous results they are having in their contacts with the beyond, grew even deeper. Jules works for the Ministry of Justice in Luxembourg as an attorney and was given special time off by his department to spend with his overseas guests. Jules's supervisor knows and approves of his involvement with transcommunication and was pleased that we had come to his country for a personal meeting with the Fischbachs.

As Maggie and I got to know each other better, we found we had much in common. She teaches school and has a class of five- and six-year-olds. Before I retired from teaching I had taught first grade for fourteen years. In another way our paths were strangely parallel. She learned about voice recordings from reading *Handbook of Psi Discoveries* by Sheila Ostrander and Lynn Schroeder, as I had.

The last two days of our stay took on an international aspect. Ernst Senkowski, whom I already knew, since he had accepted my invitation to speak at the second national conference of AA–EVP, came from West Germany accompanied by his wife, Adelheid. Tina Laurent, mentioned in Chapter 15, and her husband, Carl, arrived from Wales. Also present was Jean Paul Seyler, a Luxembourg engineer who frequently takes part in recordings, and Benedict Weis, a young Luxembourg housewife, mother and sculptress, who Technician has said has important energies to contribute to recording sessions.

Maggie had told Technician, several days before our visit, that we would be coming. He had answered that he would bring people to speak to us Friday evening as well as Saturday morning. After an enjoyable lunch together at a nearby restaurant the ten of us gathered around a large table in the Fischbach apartment to discuss the voices and to listen to various voice tapes Maggie had recorded.

One of my first questions was whether the Fischbachs are able to communicate with Technician and others from Life Stream when they are away from their apartment. I was assured that the location seemed to make no difference. At times Jules and Maggie have visited other countries using the equipment of their hosts, along with a few specialized pieces of their own designed from Technician's suggestions. On each occasion Technician and others have come through with clear messages.

Ernst Senkowski explained: "It seems successful communication depends more on the mental or psychic state of the Fischbachs than the system." He also said that he had asked Technician once: "Please tell us what is necessary to communicate with you."

Technician replied, *"You have a person on Earth, an experimenter, with special faculties and equipment, and on the other side in the transregions, there is another entity with his faculties and his equipment, and these combine and are necessary to establish the contact."*

One of the tapes Maggie played for us during this time was a recording made when Walter and Mary Jo Uphoff from Wisconsin had visited them a few weeks earlier.

Henri Sainte-Claire Deville, a frequent communicator from the other side, gave a scientific discourse lasting several minutes about space, the universe, reality, energy, and awareness. A biographical sketch of Deville can be found in Volume 6 of the 1967 edition of Collier's Encyclopedia.

Following Deville's discourse, Technician spoke to the Uphoffs directly: *"We believe, Walter Uphoff, that you believe in the existence of extraterrestrials. This is certainly correct. There are extraterrestrials. They are observing the planet Earth. Read the book* The 12th Planet *by Sitchin."*

Since returning from Luxembourg I have obtained a copy of *The 12th Planet* (published by Avon in 1978) and found it excellent and thought-provoking.

At seven that evening we all moved to the Fischbachs' recording room, a room about ten feet by twelve. It is very compact, with many open as well as built-in shelves, and contains all their taping equipment.

When using the GA 1 system, Technician has repeatedly warned that two-way communications should not be recorded because of possible dangerous space-time distortions from contact with other dimensions. Since we had a large group, Technician had said they would come through the Eurosignal-Bridge, in which taping restrictions do not apply. Each of us had our own portable tape recorders so we would have a record of everything received from the other side. After turning on the equipment, Jules turned the FM dial slightly on a small radio until the Eurosignal was heard. In less than a minute Technician's voice spoke clearly:

> *"Contact. You have contact. This is contact."*

Immediately after this came the following message:

> *"Good evening. This is Konstantin Raudive. Dear friends, we are very honored that (you have come), especially the two families Estep and Laurent. You have done much for transcommunication in English-speaking countries. A member of Life-Line would speak to you on a question that is of interest to all mankind. It is the question why some people try to make you believe there is a person like the devil."*

Technician: *"A member of Life-Line speaking from Time-Stream."*

There followed a full five-minute discourse from Sainte-Claire Deville about the church, the devil, and related matters, which I will quote in part.

> *"My name is Henri Sainte-Claire Deville. I am speaking to you beyond the finite and in the name of my group Life-Line the scientists. Dear colleagues, the devil did not exist until the Church invented him for all (those) that opposed the doctrines of the Church. . . . The leaders who perpetrated the deed through firm religious convictions really believed they were performing a useful and sacred function. Not in evil was the devil conceived but in ignorance and human weakness. . . . Without the evil one the good forces would not stand out as such. . . . Nothing would keep the community as much in line as fear of the devil. Pure and simple blackmail, the threat of spending eternity in hell as depicted ultimately by the Church was the alternative to being a good Christian. . . . Man had little choice but to obey the doctrines of the Church. After all, he couldn't be sure that such hell didn't exist—no one as having been there has re-*

turned. Nowadays we know the possibilities of transcommunication. We can tell you what it is like here on our side. Dear friends, dear colleagues, there is no hell. There is only the hell that man creates himself. So much for the reason why the devil came into the world. To this day there are some people, particularly the more fundamentalist traits, who still believe quite literally in the existence of the devil as a person. . . . Such strange beliefs are important parts of their faith. When they arrive here, they are astonished."

This ended the communication from Sainte-Claire Deville. His discourse was given in English, as well as Raudive's greeting at the beginning, out of respect for the Laurents and us, since we understand only English. Six of the other eight people in the group were fluent in English, so they had no difficulty in following.

Technician then returned and indicated he had another contact who wished to speak. A short message was given to Ernst Senkowski in German, and then the communicator turned his attention to Jean Paul Seyler. Jean Paul has serious back problems and was in a good deal of pain the entire time we were together. The unseen entity was aware of this and, still speaking in German, the common language of eight in our gathering, recommended to Jean Paul that he get a certain kind of medicine. This was a medicine unknown to all of us, but when Jean Paul checked with the local pharmacy later that evening the druggist assured him such medicine was available on special order.

As I discovered later this was not the first time Technician had given helpful medical advice. The day after returning home I called a man I know, a scientist, who is vitally interested in the Fischbachs' work, and reported to him what had taken place during our visit. When I told him about Jean Paul's message, Jim said that a few months earlier his wife had a stroke. Her condition was grave, and the doctors had little hope for her recovery. During this time Technician came through to the Fischbachs and said that Jane should start drinking a certain medicinal tea each day. Unfortunately, in spite of all efforts to locate it in this country, it was nowhere to be found. The Fischbachs finally located it in Europe and sent a supply to Jane. As soon as she began taking it daily, her condition improved, and now, although not completely recovered, she is able to spend several hours each day at her desk. Jim shared, "I'm sure other factors also contributed to her return to reasonable health, but we feel the tea played an important part."

After our successful evening recording we had much to discuss about the taping and about the voices in general.

A system, similar to the Fischbachs', is now being used by a group in Darmstadt, West Germany. This is located near Mainz, where the Senkowskis live, and Ernst has visited them and observed several recordings, during which a personal message had come through for him. The Darmstadt group has an unseen entity who acts something like Technician for the Fischbachs. This entity calls himself A B X Juno: A—coming from the other side; B—biological; X—experiment; and Juno is his special name. These contacts are recent and, although interesting, cannot yet begin to compare with what is taking place in Luxembourg.

During our discussion Maggie played several more segments of tapes received from Technician and the group he represents. In one an entity who has spoken often and who gave the personal message for me when the group from Vienna was visiting, spoke to Maggie and said she should phone Ernst Senkowski and tell him, *"The mahatmas are a reality."*

When the message was received, neither of the Fischbachs had ever heard the word *mahatma* and didn't know what it meant. It was explained to them that very great souls of past centuries have continued their development after death and gained more enlightenment. This group is sometimes referred to as the White Brotherhood (a term with which the Fischbachs were also unfamiliar). These advanced souls exist now on the highest planes and are aware and concerned about all that takes place in our own world and other planes of existence.

A world-class physicist, Dr. Burkhard Heim from West Germany, had visited the Fischbachs for the first time the weekend before we arrived. Several successful recordings were made, and he had received personal messages. In one that Maggie played for us at this time, Technician spoke to Dr. Heim and told him not to be afraid, they were going to measure his brain waves, and a loud burst of noise would be heard. Sure enough, an almost overwhelming sound swamped the recording system that lasted for several seconds and evidently resulted from the brain wave measurement. Dr. Heim left Luxembourg thoroughly convinced of the genuineness of the voices and is going to continue research and development of transcommunication.

Some months earlier Technician had told the Fischbachs they would meet a physicist who was almost blind and badly crippled in his hands. This man, through his genius, would eventually develop a system whereby all humans could communicate with those beyond death. Dr. Heim appears to be the man to whom Technician referred. He has about ten percent vision left and only a few fingers on his hands—the result of an explosion in his laboratory during the war when he was working with von Braun on the development of the German rockets.

A very real question all along has been how our "voiceless" contacts from the world of spirit are able to speak actual words that can be heard by us and that register on oscilloscopes and other electronic equipment. Technician has explained that their thoughts go through a sort of system that sets up oscillations and in turn is relayed to us, which we can pick up through our tape recorders and in a few rare cases, such as with the Fischbachs, over wall speakers. We are, in effect, hearing their thoughts in transcommunication (EVP). Technician himself uses something like a computer system with a memory containing the syllables or phonemes of all our languages. When he speaks to us, he draws upon this system to express what he wants to say. At times he is unable to find the special word he wants, for it is not in the system, and then he must substitute another word. Technician has told us that although he is an actual entity, and not a robot, the system he uses could be compared to a robot.

After breakfast the following morning our same group of ten came together at the Fischbachs. The three engineers in our party were discussing technical aspects of the phenomena, and others were talking about the philosophical-psychological impact of the voices on them personally and on society in the future. While conversation swirled around us Maggie, Jules, and I talked further. Maggie told me Technician has said she and Jules are as one and that in another dimension they *are* one. I mentioned to Maggie that this was similar to what Seth had said in the Seth books by Jane Roberts—that we could live on a conscious level in several different realities at one time. Immediately Maggie and Jules's faces brightened, and Maggie said, "Seth. Ah, yes, Seth! Technician said we should get that book and read it!" When I asked if they had, Jules answered they had just gotten it and he was starting to read it and Maggie plans to do so soon. Maggie also told me that according to Technician she and Jules had been together in a previous lifetime. During those lives they have not been together they have always felt incomplete and have searched for each other, not really knowing or understanding what was missing from that particular life.

Maggie is a practicing Roman Catholic, and when I asked how the local church felt about her work, she shrugged her shoulders and said there was no problem. She was especially pleased when Father Andreas Resch, a professor at the Lateran University, the Vatican, visited them in May. Several successful recordings were held, and Father Resch told the Fischbachs, "Our aims are quite the same."

Although some individual churches might disagree vehemently with Sainte-Clair Deville's discourse the evening before about the devil, most would approve, at least in principal, with Technician's philosophies. Technician gave Father Resch the following meditation when he visited the Fischbachs

> *"O, Gracious Lord! You created mankind from the same stem (root). You decided that all should belong to the same family. In Your presence all are Your servants, all find shelter with You. All have gathered around Your table of offerings, illumined by the light of Your providence. You protect all. You give life to all. You endowed each one with talents and abilities. All is submerged in the ocean of Your compassion. Give that we all become united, that religions become harmonized, UNITED nations, so they regard themselves as a family with the entire universe as their home. You are the power and the strength. You are forgiving and overlook shortcomings. Perhaps the time will come when our dimensions will meet."*

Few churches, Christian or otherwise, would find fault with this meditation. Some, however, might not accept Technician's comments about God given at another time. *"Man has shaped*

God's image according to his human conception in a human likeness. God, or the principle of God, is an essence that has no comparison. God is shaping His world and pilots every human being to where He wants him.''

Maggie said that Technician frequently refers to the Bible, especially the Old Testament. Once, talking about the Bible, he said, *''The book of books is a guidepost for mankind. Some guiding principles in this book were well adapted to the nomadic people living at the time.''*

All of these quoted comments from Technician were clearly heard through the speakers sitting on top of the Fischbachs' recording equipment. As a prediction for the future, he has indicated that an organization will soon be founded to deal exclusively with voice research. It will be comparable to the United Nations—*''Uniting new earth countries.''*

At about eleven that morning the ten of us again moved into the recording room. Technician had said earlier that he would try to bring someone to speak to us at that time. Like the evening before, the Eurosignal-Bridge was used, and we each held our portable tape recorders ready to tape anything that came through. Maggie and Benedict sat behind the table on which rested the Philips cassette tape deck the Fischbachs always use for Eurosignal tapings. Jules adjusted the dial slightly on one of the two small radios that sit on a shelf. Soon the Eurosignal was heard, and a moment after that Technician's voice came through the speaker of the second radio.

''Contact. Contact. Have contact.''

With this the deep male voice heard the evening before who had identified himself as Konstantin Raudive spoke. He first greeted us by saying, *''Good morning, dear friends. Here speaks Konstantin Raudive. Dear friends, thank you for coming once more.''* He then continued for seven minutes without interruption. Many things were touched upon, such as matter, different worlds beyond the physical and the astral planes:

> *''Beyond the astral world (there exists) yet another range of experience, the mental, and beyond that others of still finer nature responding to still more spiritual aspects of consciousness. All these rates of vibrations interpenetrate each other in the same way that solids,*

liquids, and gases are all present in a sponge filled with water."

Raudive concluded his address with:

"Dear friends, our time is limited, and the contact will be over at any moment. Our group, Time-Stream, wants to thank all of you for what you have done and for what you will do for transcommunication. It is an important task in the world, not an easy one. When I was on the other side, a human being, sometimes the voices I captured were more real than the people around me and then they became phantoms swirling in motion disappearing like the summer mists. Philosophers say a dream journey takes but a flash of time. You may travel to the ends of the earth in a heartbeat, and if you stay in that mysterious world of dreams, you die. Don't be afraid of death. It is not the end but a transition to a better, a finer world."

That ended our session with the other side, except for Technician, who returned and said, *"Contact has ended."*

Unlike the evening before, everything came through in English.

Do I believe we had the actual Konstantin Raudive addressing us? Although the voice was the same as that heard the previous night, and although this personality is one of the most frequent communicators, might he not be an impostor? This is possible, but I think not.

To start with, although entities can claim to be well-known personalities in order to catch the attention of the taper, this rarely continues beyond once or twice. There is no point to it. Most of those who speak from the beyond have enough ego left for them to want to be known for whom they are. In addition, we must consider Raudive's background. During his life he was a noted European psychologist and philosopher. If one rereads his eloquent closing remarks, one sees he mentions philosophers, but more than that, one can hear the psychologist still in him warning us not to remain in the world of dreams. He offers an insight as to what the voices meant to him while he was alive: *"Sometimes the voices I captured were more real than the*

people around me. . . . " From what I have read about Dr. Raudive, this was true. He spent many hours each day at his tape
recorder—so many that his hearing was affected, and his physician cautioned him to limit his time in listening to tapes.

As the group of us discussed the recording Tina asked Jules
if he had any evidence the entity really was Raudive. Jules replied that after they had taped him a few times, they asked him
for proof of his identity. Raudive gave them a phone number in
Switzerland and told them to call it. Jules did, having no idea to
whom they would be connected, and a female voice answered,
giving her name as Annemarie Morgenthaler. Jules explained
the reason for his call, and Annemarie, who is now a teacher,
was almost overwhelmed, telling them she had been Raudive's
secretary for more than ten years. Jules sent her copies of several
tapes in which the alleged Raudive spoke, and Annemarie responded that it was indeed his voice on the tapes.

In the short time left before we were driven to the airport to
catch our plane home, I discussed with Maggie her plans for the
future. I commented how I was afraid this constant parade of
visitors to the Fischbach home almost every weekend must be
a serious drain on her energies as well as Jules's. She admitted
this was so and that she and Jules had decided they must start
to severely limit the time they can give to guests. She feels
conflict about this. Up until now she and Jules had given tape
demonstrations every three months to the public in an open
meeting. People came, asking more and more questions, always
wanting more than she could give. Those who had lost loved
ones wanted her to bring them through on tape. "Sometimes
we were successful, sometimes not," she explained. Maggie
said they want to help others but feel it is taking too much time
and personal energy from their main purpose, which is inform-
ing people about the voices through their newsletter. As she
wrote in one of the first issues: "The spreading of this news
from beyond is desirable, even requested. Neither our relatives
nor former scientists of this earth who have passed on can build
a communication bridge from their side of the veil if the higher
forces do not want it."

A week after my return from Luxembourg I received a letter
from Ernst Senkowski. He wrote that a few minutes after he and
his wife, the Laurents, and the Fischbachs had returned to Jules
and Maggie's apartment after seeing us off at the airport, they

received word that Friedrich Jürgenson had died on October 15. They tried a GA 1 contact and asked Technician about him. Technician replied, *"One of us has come back. He accomplished his work on your side. Due to his age during his last years, he did not always speak in our sense. One of the pioneers, he went home. He will turn to new tasks. Now he is in one of those rooms he described during his lifetime to have a rest."*

Ernst concluded his letter by saying they had asked Technician if it would be possible later on to have contact with Jürgenson and their question was answered in the affirmative.

Since then, I have received additional word that the stresses of which Maggie and I spoke at the end of our visit increased even more. For a while, because of health reasons, all taping ceased and they were not sure if they would ever tape again. Jean Paul Seyler dropped out of the group. Benedict, although still regarding herself as a member of CETL, no longer wanted to be involved with the actual taping process. As Jules and Maggie struggled to regain their equilibrium, unsolicited messages again started to appear on their computer screen urging them to resume taping. Eventually they returned to their tape recorder but on a greatly modified scale. Upon advice from Technician, they stopped using the Eurosignal-Bridge and GA 1 system completely. At latest report, they are using a small radio tuned to 90 MHz, two ultra-violet lamps and a special antenna. Results are still good, with the paranormal voices continuing to be heard clearly through the speakers. Ernst Senkowski has visited them upon several occasions and had contact with a female entity who says she is in a parallel world. In a recent letter from Dr. Senkowski, he wrote that he and his wife Adelheid had visited the Fischbachs in January. This female entity said she had died a few months ago in her world that is parallel to our own. After regaining consciousness, she found a transcommunication station from which she is communicating with our world. Ernst wrote, "She seems to be a 'smart' one, talking swiftly about physical matters, and I am trying to get in a somewhat scientifically orientated dialogue with her for possible enlightenment!"

As promised in October, Friedrich Jürgenson has spoken through the Fischbach equipment several times. A week after his death, he spoke to Dr. Determeyer who was visiting and said, *"Man suffocates man!"*

We are privileged to hear from some of the great human beings of the past as they continue to share their thoughts, their wisdom and knowledge, gained from living in dimensions beyond our own. One can feel only gratitude to the Fischbachs and all other pioneers in the field of voice phenomena, who have made and will continue to make these contacts known to all.

Chapter 17—How to Communicate with the Voices

There is no single correct way to record voices from beyond. Experimenters use different methods, some close to the bizarre, and yet those in the next world continue to speak. They seem to do so almost in spite of us.

We won't delve into the strange, unusual ways some researchers claim to produce voices. Rather, we will look at the procedures followed more commonly by those who are noted for their clear voice tapes. Unfortunately each method has its drawbacks, and we will need to be aware of these.

I always urge everyone beginning work in the area of electronic voice phenomena to try various experiments, to see what works best, and then, after a trial-and-error period, to choose one or two ways that bring the most satisfactory results.

In my search I have tried all known procedures, as well as inventing some of my own. For months I went from one method to another, devising unique ways I hoped would bring success. Now and then an unknown friend would have something to say on tape, but this was limited. Finally in desperation I asked, "Do you like all of the things I've been trying?"

"Actually, no" came the first Class A response I'd had in weeks.

So it goes. I feel the time spent in experimental apprenticeship was not wasted. It taught me many things, and while a

number were intangible, I have always had a special fondness
for and belief in what is intangible.

Before you begin your first experiment there is certain equipment you will need. Some of the things you may already have;
if so, use them. As mentioned in Chapter 1, I began with old
equipment that only half worked, and yet voices spoke. All this
equipment has since been replaced, but not until I was positive
I wanted to work seriously in the field. I never recommend
spending a great deal of money. To start with, it isn't necessary.
Voices have been taped on the most inexpensive as well as expensive recorders, and sometimes it is difficult to tell which
came from which.

Assuming you have no equipment for experimenting, the following is what you will need before you sit down the first time
and say "Hello, is anyone here?"

1. *Tape recorder*. This will be your largest expenditure.
Whether to buy a cassette or an open-reel tape deck is the first
decision. When I replaced the recorder I used for the first month,
I bought a solid-state stereo cassette tape deck. A satisfactory
one may cost a hundred dollars, while the least expensive open-
reel recorder can cost close to six hundred. Whatever type of
tape recorder you use, and this includes a small battery-
operated tape recorder, be sure it has a counter. A counter
shows you where you are on the tape as you record, as well
as when you play the tape back later. Without a counter it is
very difficult to relocate a message.

Most individuals who work extensively with the electronic
voice usually tape on open-reel recorders, because they feel the
fidelity is better and it's more convenient. This is what I use,
but I have never regretted buying a cassette deck. Excellent
voices came through, and most of the methods I follow today
were developed while taping with it. I continue to use it for
making duplicate tapes to send to my friends.

There is one caution about starting with a cassette recorder:
Although some experimenters report good results with built-in
condenser mikes, they are, for the most part, noisy, and their
use will in almost every case lead to great discouragement. Unless you are unusually fortunate your voices will initially be faint
whispers. In a contest between a noisy condenser mike and the
voices, the mike will win, and you won't hear a thing. If you

already have a cassette recorder with a built-in mike, there is frequently a place where an external microphone can be plugged in. When this is done, the built-in mike automatically becomes disconnected.

2. *Microphone*. There is some question as to whether a microphone is absolutely necessary for recording voices. I have made recordings without them and never picked up a thing. The voices who speak to me have said they need a microphone, so I provide one. In addition, by using a microphone, my own voice is on tape, which provides a record of what I have said.

The microphone I like best and use all the time is an electric condenser mike that requires a small battery. You can spend less, or more, but as long as it is quiet and sensitive, you should get good results.

Ten years ago I went to the hardware store and bought a seventy-five-cent metal funnel. I slipped the neck over the microphone head, the wide open part facing out. It seemed to act as a megaphone for those who speak, and their voices improved immediately. I have never taken it off.

3. *Headphones*. Don't think about attempting to listen to EVP voices unless you have a set of headphones. At the beginning you may pick up a voice every two or three weeks that can be heard without their use, but you'll miss many soft voices if you don't wear them. Even today I still use headphones every time I play a tape back. If the voice sounds loud and clear, I will take off the headphones and play the message over the wall speaker to see if it can still be heard.

There are different types of headphones that can be used. I would recommend the earmuff kind, which fit tightly over and enclose the ears. They do a better job of shutting out the extraneous sounds than the models that merely cover the ear.

4. *Amplifier*. Since a tape deck, whether it be a cassette or open-reel one, doesn't have its own amplifier, this means connecting it to an external one. There is a wide range in prices. While it isn't necessary to spend hundreds of dollars, the cheapest may not do the job or have the various refinements you might want.

I have had several and finally settled on a solid-state stereo unit with bass and treble controls, master switch, left-right balance, and so on. It has 480 watts at full power, which is more than sufficient. The problem with amplification is that the more you try to amplify voices, the more you amplify background noise.

5. *Wall speaker*. I use a wall speaker mainly as an aid in classifying the clearer voices and in determining which ones are Class A. The speaker is also convenient when others come to listen to my duplicate tapes of Class A voices.

6. *Stereo frequency equalizer with individual controls*. This isn't necessary but is a nice addition if you plan to spend much time working with voice phenomena. It helps tailor the responses you receive so you can get the most out of your recording system. With it you can bring out many fainter voices that would otherwise be missed.

7. *Tape*. Whether you use a cassette or open-reel recorder, you will want to choose your tape carefully. Low noise, high sensitivity tape is best. While you don't need the most expensive, the cheapest is usually a poor investment. If you are recording on a cassette recorder, it is a good idea not to use a tape over sixty minutes long. The longer tapes sometimes get wrapped around the spindles while recording or while rewinding, and portions of the tape may be destroyed while you are trying to untangle them.

Now that you have all your equipment, where should you put it? I am fortunate in having an office in my home where I work. In my previous home I took one end of the basement, put up two folding screens, one at each side, and presto—an office! With the addition of a desk and some other furniture, I was in business.

We moved into our present home several years ago, and there is a room off the sunroom that I converted to an office. The first time I made a recording from the new location a number of messages came through.

Choose the quietest area of your home, as distant from the comings and goings of family and friends as possible, and go to work. Don't move around. While the voices will speak anywhere, always try to make it as easy as possible for them. Knowing they can find you at the same place, at the same time, seems to cause less confusion in establishing regular contact with the other side.

This brings up the question of scheduling. Here again, voices will come through anytime, day or night, but I feel, especially at first, it is wise to follow a fixed schedule. Since I am a morning person and my energy level is highest then, that is when I do the majority of my recordings. I suggest you choose the best time for you and also make your contacts when you are least likely to be interrupted by family and friends.

Once those on the other side learn where and when you tend to record, chances are they'll be there.

A great deal has been said about the mechanics of recording, which I will touch on in a few moments, but not enough attention has been given to technique.

Technique, within the framework of EVP, denotes the development of a relationship between the experimenter and those voices who wish to communicate through a tape recorder.

By this time I hope I have been able to show that personal relationships can be formed with those in other dimensions. Much will depend on how seriously you enter into voice recording, your personal feelings about the phenomena, and how much you want this relationship to evolve.

As with earth-plane acquaintances, how far you progress in this relationship is largely up to you. If you limit it to an occasional "Hello, how are you?" whether with the incarnate or discarnate, you'll not get very far. To have meaningful relationships, here and beyond, you have to work at them.

Courtesy and consideration should be extended to all those who exhibit an inclination to communicate. Respect their wish not to speak when they indicate this. Since they are sensitive personalities, with feelings, we must be aware of their needs and allow for their individual differences.

Although the voices occasionally criticize me, I never criticize back. Usually their criticism has been justified and, admitting they were right, there was little I could say. If I felt misjudged by them, and this has happened only once or twice, I tried to explain my position and went on from there.

They know they are free to say whatever they wish to me. I do not make judgments of individuals for what they say or do.

That is not meant to indicate I love everyone unreservedly, for I don't. People are what they are because of what they have had to live through before they get to me. When those on the other side express that they like or love me, I reply in kind and assure them of my deep, warm affection for them. When they say they hate me, I tell them I am sorry they feel this way and hope that someday they won't. My background as a social worker, camp director, and educator has made me unusually perceptive about people, and this has carried over in my contacts with worlds beyond.

When we work with the discarnate we need to keep in mind that their human personalities have survived essentially intact from the physical plane. If we suspect that we may be communicating with entities who are not of the spirit world, then courtesy and consideration should still be our watchwords.

A frequent complaint about the voices is that they say little of import. The reasons for this can be many. We, as researchers of the phenomena, must carefully consider our questions. If we don't ask anything of consequence, how can we expect much to come back? Too many experimenters, I am afraid, treat their communicants on the other side like retarded five-year-old children. If the voices respond in kind, the blame is ours. Some of those who speak to me have kept my own intellectual capacities scrambling to keep up, and at times they have left me behind.

Recordings should not stretch on indefinitely but should be limited. Five minutes at a time is sufficient. Later you may extend this somewhat, but even today, I keep my recordings under ten minutes. Playback takes a long time. A five-minute recording can easily take thirty minutes to replay.

Everyone has to work out his or her own techniques for communicating. You will want to ask those questions that interest you most. As a rule, I try to explore one area at a time, whether for one recording or ten. Frequently at the end of a recording I will request that the voices bring to me a particular individual for the next recording. Often this individual then indicates his presence in the next recording.

At other times I will say that I want to explore a certain area i.e., how the various entities get through to us, how they detect our voices, and so on.

During a five-minute recording I may ask three or four questions, allowing about a minute of blank tape to run between each question. Although most voices now answer, if they're going to at all, within ten to fifteen seconds, by permitting a longer time for them to come through, you needn't worry about cutting off someone who is making an effort to respond. The ability to speak to us from the other side is something many entities seem to have to learn. I believe in giving them all the help and encouragement possible.

As mentioned, voices will at first be faint and difficult to hear. Many will whisper, and unless you listen for this, you'll think nothing has been recorded. It is a strange fact in voice recordings that the longer you work in the area, and the more effort you put into it, the more voices you will encounter, and, to a certain extent, the better the quality will be. Those voices who now speak to me for the first time rarely do so in whispers. While learning how to do it is still a factor on their part, it seems that once you have been "tagged" by those in charge of recordings, there are helpers standing by to help the neophytes over there.

Proper playback technique is something the experimenter has to learn. It is here that many throw their hands up in despair and go on to something else. Wearing headphones, with the amplifier turned up as high as possible without causing discomfort to the ears, play a five-minute segment over at least several times. You will hear a soft hissing called "white noise" in the background. Many times the voices will be lost in this noise, and you must learn how to distinguish the voices from the background sounds. If you think a voice may be speaking, stop the recording and play that segment over and over. With repeated playback, if there is a voice, its message may become at least partly clear.

At the same time you must be careful not to want to hear voices too much. This very desire can create voices when none are there. Some experimenters will take a tiny portion of tape on which they think they hear a voice, and play it over a hundred times. It is not surprising if at the end of that time they are convinced they have something. My policy is to play back a segment that seems to contain a voice six or seven times. If at the end of seven playbacks I have been unable to interpret what is there, I proceed with the rest of the playback. While undoubtedly I miss some messages this way, I would rather do this than create something out of nothing.

When I am sure I have a paranormal voice message, I enter it into my log. Everyone who works at all seriously with electronic voice phenomena should develop a good record-keeping system for experiments and results. A spiral-ring notebook makes a good log. As soon as a message is recorded, the date, time, the number on the counter where the message is heard, the message itself, and the question asked, should be entered into the log. The tape should be properly labeled, with the reel number and track to correspond with the log included.

As an example from my own log: Reel 22-Track 3-October 27-9:15 A.M.-Counter 562: *"Is still not standing this one."* (Bill, are you standing by?)

I write notes above some of the messages that are of special interest to me. For instance, I classified the above message as Class A and noted that it was given in a clear voice.

Keeping a log takes some time, but you can simplify it. By noting the counter on a tape where you have recorded a message and the message given, you can relocate it quickly to play over for yourself or others who may come to listen to your recordings.

In familiarizing yourself with the mechanics of recording, keep in mind that voices have been clearly recorded in each of the ways to be discussed.

When I first began to record, I used the straight-microphone method. None of the methods are difficult to master, but microphone recordings are the simplest, most direct, and least controversial mode of recording the taped voice.

In a microphone recording, all you need to do is plug the mike into the microphone jack of the tape recorder and start to record. Many experimenters use this method all the time, and occasionally they will get a clear Class A voice.

In my own work, after a few months I became dissatisfied with the microphone method. The voices were faint and difficult to distinguish above the white noise in the background. There might be one or two Class A voices every week or so to keep me from becoming entirely discouraged, but I wanted more than that. The messages given were also extremely short. One or two words were the rule and consisted basically of *"come here,"* *"help me,"* and *"cold."* While it was exciting to get even this much from the next dimension, I didn't feel I was learning much about the world beyond.

Possibly, if I had continued with the microphone method, the voices would in time have improved in quality and been able to give longer messages, but if there was a better way, I wanted to try to find it.

Since I was dissatisfied with what I was getting, and at the same time couldn't help but feel the voices were capable of much more, given the proper help, I began searching for better methods.

Dr. Konstantin Raudive used the diode extensively for his recordings. When I read that he received excellent voices with many five- and six-word messages, I decided to experiment with a diode.

The diode is a simple, broad-band, crystal-diode radio detector and can be easily built by anyone with some electronic know-how. It is about twice the size of a matchbox, with two inches of wire sticking out of one end that acts as an antenna, and a wire at the other end that can be plugged into the microphone input of the recorder.

Diode recordings, as far as I am concerned, have a number of drawbacks. The antenna picks up many radio broadcasts. Although you can shorten the antenna, which will help reduce radio reception, if you shorten it too much, paranormal voices will also be eliminated.

While it is true that I have sometimes recorded excellent, clear voices with a diode, these instances were rare indeed. Three-word messages were the maximum I received using this method, with one or two words predominating. Most of the voices, quality-wise, were no better than when I used the straight-microphone method.

The interfrequency method was developed by Friedrich Jürgenson. Since he was considered the "master" by many experimenters in the field of the electronic voice, I decided to see if his method would work for me.

Jürgenson would tune his radio to a weak, middle-pitched humming sound, which, in his area, is found at 1480 KHz on the standard AM broadcast band. Similar signals can be received in the United States in the 1650 KHz band.

This method was developed to such an extent by Jürgenson that he could supposedly set the volume of his radio at a comfortably loud level and hear the voices speaking to him through the radio. As a result, he could respond instantly to them and have extended two-way conversations with those on the other side. For best results with weak voices, he preferred to couple the radio directly with the tape deck and to monitor the voices with his headphones.

In my own experiments with the interfrequency method I met with indifferent success. While the results were better than with the diode, in that when the voices did speak they were usually Class A, for the most part I received nothing.

Comparing the three methods, straight-microphone, diode, and interfrequency, I found that the microphone method worked best for me. Quantity-wise I received three times as many messages, and though the voices were still faint and brief, at least they were there.

With all my many hours of experience making the recordings, one thing became clear: The voices used sounds to help in their voice manifestations. I had been told that complete silence was of utmost importance in voice recordings. No one dare sniffle, stretch, shift position, or make any noise whatsoever for fear any extraneous sound would be interpreted as a voice message. The reason is obvious: The voices are so faint and far between at the beginning, it is easy to credit them for speaking when they are not even present. A sniffle could become *"Hello there,"* when it is nothing more than a plain sniffle.

Still, I found that the *swish, swish* of car tires going by outside on a wet road would often result in a Class A voice. Water running in the kitchen would produce additional voices. At times the voices even seemed to create their own background noises to help them speak.

I began deliberately making controlled sounds while I was recording. We won't go into all of the experiments I tried, for while each produced voices, none were outstanding. The one exception seemed to be when I played a record on the record player. When voices spoke then, they were loud and clear, and gave longer and more interesting messages. They were, though, still infrequent.

About this time Raymond Cass and I exchanged letters and tapes. I was favorably impressed with his tapes, and when he described his method of using the air-band for background noise, I decided to try it.

As soon as I began making air-band recordings, I noticed a dramatic increase in both the quantity and quality of the voices. It was as if the various entities had been waiting for me to use this mode of recording, and as soon as I did, they responded better than I could ever have hoped.

This is basically the way I do most of my recording today, with a few changes. Instead of setting the tuner of my radio to one spot on the air-band and leaving it, I slowly turn the dial back and forth between 125 and 127 MHz. There is a slight wave effect as a result, and at one point static. The voices, using the sounds produced by the static as well as the waving, come in clearly. Frequently I can hear them speaking through the radio, but usually it isn't until playback that I can interpret what they have said. Once in a while, the voices will be loud enough to hear as messages come through. When this occurs, I respond immediately to them, not having to wait until playback; they in their turn may then answer me.

Skeptics of electronic voice phenomena are delighted when you tell them you record paranormal voices through the radio. "All your voices are from radio broadcasts," they insist.

I would be less than honest if I said this never happens, for it does. At times I will hear the air control tower reporting to Whiskey that he is free to land, or instructing Zebra to take flight path such and such. I recognize them for what they are and do not think I have a paranormal voice.

On the other hand I cannot believe that a radio program speaks to me personally by calling me *"Estep"* or that I have an unknown admirer somewhere taking up the airwaves and declaring his love for me. In all normal radio broadcasts I have never heard such unusual grammatical sentence structure or such a unique way of expressing ideas as with those who speak from beyond.

To me one of the most convincing arguments to prove that these are authentic voices from another dimension and not a radio broadcast is the way they answer my questions. If you check back over the hundreds of examples I have given, you will see that from the content of many of the messages, as well as the context in which they were used, they must have originated from another plane of existence. If I have any question about the paranormality of a message I don't play it for others or even talk about it.

As I mentioned in the first chapter, I rate each message as A, B, or C. The A messages, the loudest and clearest, are usually interpreted the same way by most people who hear them. Class B messages are also reasonably clear and like the Class A messages can be heard without headphones. They may require four or five playings before the message is interpreted, and there is usually more disagreement among those who listen to them than with Class A, about what is said. Class C messages always require headphones and out of four or five words, normally not more than two or three can be interpreted.

Would the voices have come through as loudly and clearly twelve years ago as they do now, if I had used the air-band from the start? My feeling is that the experimenter must work diligently to contact the other side before the voices respond in kind. He needs to prove his sincerity and that his or her reasons for trying to communicate are commendable. He has to first gain the attention of those who are in charge of recordings on the other side, and once having gained it, must show that he can be trusted to present the story of the world beyond death in a forthright manner. Developing a good relationship, as mentioned earlier, takes time. It is something that cannot be rushed.

Since many experimenters work for weeks before picking up their first word, I was fortunate to record *"beauty"* on the sixth day. Even with this, it was far from easy. I would go for days and not hear a thing and then, when I was feeling most discouraged, someone would come through and say, *"Don't give up."* I think this is one of the secrets of voice recordings. If you don't give up, if you persevere, you will receive answers. The voices will speak to those who search, but it is up to each person to initiate that search.

We would be remiss if we didn't also consider the moral and social responsibilities we as communicators in the electronic voice field have to others as well as to ourselves.

Someone working in the area of EVP needs to be constantly aware of what can happen as a result of what he claims he has received on tape. In this he must hope to have the wisdom to know when to keep silent. My own guideline is simple: If I think it would cause harm or grief to someone, I say nothing; if I am not sure, I still say nothing.

Once a visitor of mine called upon the late leader of an international consciousness movement whom she had known. She asked him what he thought of the present leader of the movement. An answer was received, but we were unable to interpret it. The following day, after several playbacks, his reply became clear, and it was an uncomplimentary one. This was not shared with the woman who had asked the question. No good purpose would have been served, and conceivably it could have caused harm.

If a spirit voice indicates unhappiness in the spirit world, should you tell his or her family of your contact on the tape recorder?

You will never be allowed to stop with the good news that the loved one still survives. The person's family will, if they accept the concept at all, want to know what the individual said, and then will press to hear the message for themselves. It doesn't take much imagination to realize what the words, *"Help me to come back,"* could do to those remaining. Common sense dictates not to mention those spirits who have not found happiness.

More difficult to decide is whether you should tell those concerned that you have heard from someone they loved, when that person has said he or she is happy. Even when the news is good, the issue needs to be approached cautiously.

The first thing you must have is strong, clear Class A voices on tape. Having that, you must try to determine how the family will react. Contrary to what you might think, not everyone is happy about the idea of spirit communication.

Some people have a negative reaction, perhaps rooted in superstitious fear, when they consider that the dead are still actively around and can speak. When this is related to one they loved, their unwillingness to accept the voices is intensified.

If you feel this will not be a problem with the family in question and that only good will come from your sharing the information with them, you must next decide how they should be approached. This suggests a time when just you and the person or persons involved can be alone together. Be as gentle, as tactful, as possible. If they ask to hear the tape, you must be prepared to play it for them. The family should be told that the voice may sound different from the way they remember it. They also need to be as ready as possible for what could be a moving experience.

In addition to the responsibility we have to others, we have one to ourselves. It has been said by many, and rightly so, that not everyone should become involved with the paranormal. Time and again I have read and heard in lectures that unless you know what you're doing, dabbling around in the various areas of what is considered paranormal is similar to a child playing with dynamite.

Before beginning experiments with the Ouija board, automatic writing, electronic voice phenomena, or anything else considered paranormal, be sure that you have a firm grip on reality. Voice phenomena work can, by its very nature, give immense personal satisfaction, but it can also take the greatest toll on an individual emotionally.

Will you be able to accept what may come through? If you call on loved ones and they beg you for help and tell you they are unhappy, what will you do? You will reach out to help, but there is only so much you can do, and unless you possess great faith, you may feel it is not enough.

Almost as difficult to live with is possible rejection from those you still love. When the person called upon doesn't respond, is it a technical problem or a lack of interest? You will hope it is technical, but there is always a kernel of fear that they may no longer care. If they respond with, *"I hate you"* or *"Go away,"* how will it affect you? Even though you can't be sure who has spoken you'll probably wonder whether it was the one you loved.

How real is the danger of spirit possession? The spirits themselves don't seem completely sure about it. When I asked if there was such a thing as possession I received three different answers within ten seconds: *"Yes!"* *"There's not."* *"Don't know."*

The following morning, hoping for a single answer, I asked the same question again. This time someone said *"Yes"* in an echo effect. During this same recording I had queried why, if possession was a fact, a spirit would try to do this. Two answers came back: *"He's not big enough"* and two counters later, *"He's not good enough."* I interpret this to mean that undesirable spirit personalities with a "smallness" of soul may attempt possession.

It appears that under certain conditions a susceptible person may become possessed. Possession need not be bad. We accept more readily a person's gift for healing, but that, too, might be a case of temporary possession. Genuine healers make no claim of healing; instead, they consider themselves "instruments" of God, a channel God uses and through which He performs His miracles. According to that outlook, I think we must also accept that an undesirable entity can take over a human personality.

The difficulty is in ascertaining who is susceptible, which is an uncertain venture at best.

Excitable, impressionable, easily frightened individuals should stay away from paranormal experiments. Those who are insecure and uncertain about themselves should also avoid the paranormal as much as possible.

The danger of obsession may be more real than the danger of possession. Your tape recorder may come to exert the call of a siren on you. If it becomes the most important thing in your life, exercise caution: there is danger in permitting it to become all-consuming. Be wary also of journeying off on an ego trip, as some experimenters do. Retaining a sense of humor and remembering who you are will help keep recording voices in its proper perspective.

If you are positive the voices are genuine, be prepared to defend your conviction of their authenticity against skeptics. This doesn't mean becoming combative with those who scoff at what you do. While you may disagree with individuals who feel it is utterly impossible to engage in any kind of postmortem or otherworldly communication, don't take it upon yourself to play missionary to change their convictions. When necessity demands that you speak, do so in a calm, assured manner. Invite those who have forced the confrontation to listen to some of your tapes. Whether the invitation is accepted or declined, it will show your willingness to put your beliefs and your evidence to a test. Any field of endeavor is frequently judged by those actively engaged in it. Try to keep this in mind if you are called on to support electronic voice phenomena.

The responsibility of our communication with the voices is two-pronged. Let us neither forget the physical realm we are still a part of nor dismiss our involvement with those who speak to us on tape because they are of another world. We owe every world our sincerest, most honest, efforts.

Chapter 18—The Voices Tell Us How and Why They Communicate

> Your soul is not defeated. —Unknown entity speaking from the world beyond death

Like us, those in the next dimension communicate in different ways.

Many of them insist *"I shout"* when asked how they are able to speak to us. The "shouters" do, in fact, sound as if they are shouting, yet the means enabling the spirits to communicate at all seems more involved than that.

James is the person, you may remember, who, one evening when I asked if he was standing by, replied, *"The faithful still have it."* I had heard "You are cleared for landing" through my radio. On tape playback this was what I expected to hear, but whoever controls recordings in the unseen world obliterated the air controller's words and substituted others. This sort of phenomenon occurs frequently in voice messages. I found it interesting, but perhaps of no significance, that the message had the same number of syllables as the censored one from the air control tower.

Since I like to be as precise as possible, I continually interrogate the spirits about how they are able to communicate with the earth plane. Many answers have been returned. I mentioned in Chapter 10 a confusing one about entering a vacuum. Some other replies have fortunately been more easily understood.

We saw in the last chapter how the voices utilize extraneous sounds in our environment as an important aid for communication with us, frequently employing even just their rhythm.

Those in other dimensions may also use the experimenter's energies, in addition to the extraneous sounds, to assist them. Some tapers report feeling "drained" after recording. This hasn't been my experience; in fact, after a successful recording session I typically feel like I've been pepped up by a handful of vitamin pills. I have thought these experiences of either tiredness or invigoration may be more of a psychological than a physiological condition. It is also possible that I receive some of the energies of the unseen. Olga Worrall claimed she used the energies of those from the beyond during her healing services.

The first time I asked how they communicated with us, the word *"ectoplasm,"* was taped. I felt certain I had misheard the message. The word "ectoplasm" had a dubious connotation to me, one where I conjure up reports of mediums speaking in spectral voices through veils of cobwebby material, purportedly ectoplasm, floating here and there; later on, the ectoplasm would prove to be nothing more than a swatch of cheesecloth.

In the next recording I told the spirits that I thought I'd misunderstood their message and reiterated my question. Again the word *"Ectoplasm"* was returned.

A year and a half later, when Styhe told me they didn't use a vacuum for communication, I inquired whether ectoplasm was ever used. *"Yes, that's right"* was Styhe's clear Class A answer. I then asked him what way they used most frequently to speak to us, and he replied in a partly monotone, still Class A voice, *"We adjust to it."*

This answer makes sense and simultaneously gives us a glimpse of the level of their intelligence. Like us, they don't always follow the same procedure but make allowances and adaptations according to conditions.

In September I further explored the question of their using the experimenter's energies to facilitate communication. I then evaluated if I'd had any inkling of this in my own firsthand experience: I realized that although a number of Class A messages have been recorded while I've been absent from the room, the majority, by far, come as I am sitting beside the tape recorder.

During the 9:30 A.M. recording on September fourth I asked

the spirits whether I was correct in assuming it easier for them to create voice manifestations when I am present in the recording room because they used my energy. Someone answered, *"You can throw off."*

Twenty-four hours later, referring back to the previous day's message, I asked whether what I "throw off" is a type of electrical energy. *"You're right with that"* I was told. During this same recording I also asked if the experimenter might have a magnetic type of energy. Someone replied, *"Not."*

On the morning of September sixth I requested they reaffirm their message of two days earlier about my throwing off electrical energy. A low male voice expressed, *"A good thing."* During this same recording I asked if ectoplasm is a form of electrical energy. A partly monotone, Class A voice responded with, *"Expansion probably,"* and two counts later added, *"That's right."*

Twenty-four hours later I requested they bring to me someone who could answer my questions about the energies those on the other side draw from us, the experimenters.

Within a few counters they indicated this had been done. I then asked what type of electrical energies experimenters give off. *"Meela"* was the clear reply. The dictionary doesn't reveal such a word, so this answer leaves us in the dark. It may be a type of energy with which those in the spirit world are familiar but we are not.

Last spring, when I asked how they knew when I sat down to record, someone said, *"We activate."*

Twelve hours later when I asked if I had recorded this message correctly, a female voice replied, *"Yes."*

As mentioned before, Friedrich Jürgenson, as well as Konstantin Raudive, have said there is a central transmitting agency in the next dimension that is responsible for many of the loudest and clearest voice recordings. As indicated, my questions about this have received answers in the affirmative. While it appears that many who speak to me come to my office, others seem to communicate from the agency itself.

In the spring, when I asked if some spirit communicators go to the transmitting agency to speak, a loud emphatic voice avowed, *"I do."*

In the next recording I asked why they went to the agency for recordings. Two different voices replied—the first one with

"They say," to be finished by another voice with the surprising information, *"It brings us luck."*

A month later I again inquired if spirits went to the central transmitting agency to listen and take part in recordings. I was told *"Yes, this one."*

The following day I wanted to know if there was more than one agency. A voice replied, *"There's lots of them."*

This answer received support two months later when I asked Styhe about the existence of more than one transmitting agency in the spirit world. He replied, *"There is."*

It had occurred to me, early in my tapings, that the experimenter might serve as a sort of antenna in voice recordings. When I inquried if this was a correct assumption on my part, the answer, *"This is so,"* was returned twice in a clear voice.

Two weeks later I further explored this question. I asked if the experimenter functioned like a radio or TV antenna, or a receiving station.

The reply *"Right!"* was heard over the radio. I immediately asked if this word had come from them, and someone assured me, *"It was sent on. Of thus it did."* I continued by asking if their answer meant the experimenter *does* act as an antenna to assist in the transmittal of messages from the next dimension. A loud, powerful voice boomed out, *"I did,"* and two counters later added, *"I can't say how you do that."*

This is an example of a short two-way conversation between an experimenter and those on the other side. I was also interested in, and appreciated, the spirit's honest answer when he admitted that while he knows the experimenter is akin to an antenna and receiving station, he doesn't know quite how this is accomplished. I have been fortunate that in most of my contacts with the other side, similar honesty has been shown.

I have mentioned before that there are apparently some kind of trainers in the world beyond who help those wishing to speak. The morning of September twentieth, when I asked if I had friends with me, five answers were returned within five counters on the tape recorder:

FIRST VOICE: *"Uh. Good-bye."*
SECOND VOICE: *"Now will you speak?"*
FIRST VOICE: *"Uh. Hello."*

SECOND VOICE: *"Trainer, don't cross over like that."*
FIRST VOICE: *"So I need you."*

In the second recording that morning I asked if they had trainers and teachers in the next dimension to instruct those who wish to speak to us. *"Right! That's right"* was the answer.

There have been repeated references about a line the spirits use to help them communicate. The following five messages, all Class A, are examples of this.

"Keep the line in sight" (after I asked Styhe if he was with me).

"Once I put your line out, I pick them up" (in response to my asking if there are those who want to speak but are unable to).

"Remember, I'll find you" (when I asked if they had found my line).

"These are perfect line" (in answer to my question as to what my line is).

"We speak from the line" (when I asked if an individual speaks from the line).

Several years ago I made a startling discovery. Some tapers reported receiving messages on the reverse side of their tapes. I began to listen to the reverse side of my tapes and discovered that I also have numerous good-quality voices there.

To hear messages on the other side of the tape, the experimenter should record normally. At the tape's conclusion take the two reels off the tape recorder. Turning them to the opposite side, place the right reel on the left side and the left reel on the right side. Before pushing the PLAY button, twist the tape once so it will play through from left to right with the shiny side up. It is then that the voices are heard. They are not heard when the tape is played forward in the normal way. The experimenter's voice is backward on the tape, as are any earth-plane broadcasts that broke in while the recording was being made. The paranormal voice is frequently Class A and perfectly intelligible. Although the volume of the voice is reduced slightly, the white noise is almost eliminated, which makes the voice unusually clear.

There are also voices on the reverse side of cassette tapes.

They are just as loud and just as clear as those found on the reverse side of reel to reel tapes. After making a recording on a cassette tape deck, the cassette tape is duplicated onto the reel tape. You then turn the reel tape over, following the procedure described earlier, and if paranormal voices spoke on the reverse side of the cassette tape, they will be heard.

Two weeks after I became aware there were voices on the reverse as well as the forward sides of my tapes, I asked those in the next dimension if they found any difference between one side of the tape and the other. *"We use either side,"* someone answered. I believe that when someone from another dimension speaks to us through our tape recorder, he is not able to control where his voice goes—it just goes—sometimes on one side of the tape, sometimes on the other.

Mercedes Shepanek has spoken to several experimenters a number of times since her death. Clara Laughlin once asked Mercedes about the reverse voices and Mercedes replied, *"We don't know that,"* indicating to both Clara and me, that the invisibles don't know where their voices go when they speak.

The question remains why, when it goes on the wrong side of the tape, it doesn't sound backward as the experimenter's voice does? No one has been able to answer this but my thought is that since time, space, and matter have a different meaning to those in other dimensions they are able to use without difficulty *"either side"* of the matter of magnetic recording tape. One thing seems certain, only a paranormal entity would be capable of this.

I now know that, at times, the questions I asked during a recording will be answered on the reverse side of the tape. Several paranormal entities may carry on a short conversation between themselves on the reverse side. They continue to be aware of us. The content and quality of the messages do not greatly differ between one side of the tape and the other. Interestingly, all realities I am in communication with come through clearly on the reverse side. It is unusual not to have at least two such messages each day I record and occasionally as many as ten.

Everything considered, while we have not learned as much as we would like to about how those in the next dimension reach us, we have learned something. We are moving in the right direction, and as time unfolds more will become clear. I sometimes feel that voice recordings must go through progression, through a form of evolution, and that only by experimenters proving to the worlds beyond a willingness to work within the parameters set by them, will the whole field of the electronic voice be permitted to advance.

I am willing to accept whatever conditions our communicants set for I know that eventually we will be able to find our way firmly, without hesitation or faltering, to the other side. "Crossing the bridge" is available, not only to our friends in other realms, but to those of us who wish to make the journey. That they want this to be a mutual crossing there can no longer be any doubt of. If they hadn't meant for our worlds to meet, they would not have begun to speak thirty years ago.

Recently I asked Styhe why he and his friends sought to contact us on the earth plane. His female associate first answered, *"Help them."* Two counters later Styhe agreed, clearly giving the same message, *"Help them."* In the following recording he replied, *"It is,"* when I asked whether it was accurate to think they wanted to help us so we would know what to expect when we crossed over to the spirit world.

Many months ago, when I was working on the third chapter, "The Voices on Death and Dying," a clear voice said, *"Your soul is not defeated."* They knew I was writing about death, and they took this additional way to reassure me, to reassure everyone, that life does not end at the grave. Life is eternal.

Why should any person want to meet, through a tape recorder, beings not existing in the physical plane? Knowing that the soul, the "I" in consciousness, is indestructible gives us a deeper appreciation for all life. Since we will carry our essence over to the world beyond death, perhaps we will learn to live more fully, to open ourselves to our earth-plane life. There is comfort in knowing we survive death, but survival, unless based on what is virtuous, is an empty victory.

The journey has just begun. I am convinced it will never end.

Bibliography

Bander, Peter. *Voices from the Tapes*. New York: Drake Publishers, 1973.

Beloff, John. "Voluntary Movement, Biofeedback Control and PK," *Parapsychology Review*, July–August 1979.

Ebon, Martin. *Communicating with the Dead*. New York: New American Library.

Geller, Uri. *Uri Geller: My Story*. New York: Praeger Publishers, 1975.

Leichtman, Robert. *Edgar Cayce Returns*. Columbus, Ohio: Ariel Press, 1978.

Moody, Raymond. *Life After Life*. St. Simons Island, Georgia: Mockingbird Books, 1975.

Osis, Karlis, and Erlendur Haraldsson. *At the Hour of Death*. New York: Avon Books, 1977.

Ostrander, Sheila, and Lynn Schroeder. *Handbook of Psi Discoveries*. New York: Berkley Publishing Corp., 1974.

Raudive, Konstantin. *Breakthrough*. New York: Taplinger Publishing Co., 1971.

Ring, Kenneth. *Life at Death*. New York: Coward, McCann & Geoghegan, 1980.

Rogo, D. Scott, and Raymond Bayless, *Phone Calls from the Dead*. Englewood Cliffs, N.J.: Prentice-Hall, 1979.

Smith, E. Lester. "The Raudive Voices—Objective or Subjective? A Discussion," *The Journal of the American Society for Psychical Research*, January 1974.

Stevenson, Ian. *Twenty Cases Suggestive of Reincarnation.* Charlottesville, Va.: University Press of Virginia, 1974.

Welch, William Addams. *Talks with the Dead.* New York: Pinnacle Books, 1975.

White, Stewart Edward. *The Unobstructed Universe.* New York: E. P. Dutton & Co., 1940.

About the Author

Sarah Wilson Estep is founder and president of the American Association–Electronic Voice Phenomena. She sends out a quarterly newsletter to the membership and is in touch with parapsychological researchers throughout the world. Sarah and her husband live in Severna Park, Maryland.

American Association–Electronic Voice Phenomena is an organization for all those interested in the ongoing research concerning electronic communication with other dimensions. Members are kept advised of progress through a quarterly newsletter. They have the opportunity to meet others engaged in this exciting field through national conferences and through correspondence with other members listed on a cross-country list. If they wish, they may also take an active part in the research itself.

For further information write:

AA–EVP
Box 668
Severna Park,
Maryland 21146 U.S.A.